"If good cheer is the best physician, then the best physician, I figure, is one who brings good cheer. That physician would be C.B. Skelton. If I were a doctor, I'd prescribe this book for everyone who needed cheering up. You'll laugh out loud at some of the stories. I certainly did."

Phil Hudgins
Senior Editor
Community Newspapers Inc., Athens, Ga.

When I read Dr. Skelton's book, I laughed a lot…I cried a little…and then I laughed some more.

Myles Godfrey, Publisher
The Barrow Eagle
Winder, Ga

DIRTY LAUNDRY
DON'T
TAKE NO DOCTOR'S ORDERS

DIRTY LAUNDRY
DON'T TAKE NO DOCTOR'S ORDERS

C.B. SKELTON, M.D.

ReadersMagnet, LLC

Dirty Laundry Don't Take No Doctor's Orders
Copyright © 2018 by C.B. Skelton, M.D.

Published in the United States of America
ISBN Paperback: 978-1-948864-29-9
ISBN eBook: 978-1-948864-16-9

All rights reserved. No part of this publication may be reproduced, stored in a retrieval system or transmitted in any way by any means, electronic, mechanical, photocopy, recording or otherwise without the prior permission of the author except as provided by USA copyright law.

The opinions expressed by the author are not necessarily those of ReadersMagnet, LLC.

ReadersMagnet, LLC
10620 Treena Street, Suite 230 | San Diego, California, 92131 USA
1.619. 354. 2643 | www.readersmagnet.com

Book design copyright © 2018 by ReadersMagnet, LLC. All rights reserved.
Cover Art by Sam Y. Morris
Cover design by Ericka Walker
Interior design by Shieldon Watson

DEDICATION

This collection of stories is dedicated to the loving memory of my wonderful, supportive and beloved, late wife,

Nora Louisa Hart Skelton

Without her love and encouragement, my life could never have been kept together enough to remember all these stories, much less to publish them. Nora kept me in line and never allowed me to feel sorry for myself nor to retain any excessive feelings of self-importance. She had her own way of bringing me back to reality when ego threatened to get out of hand or self-pity reared its head.

Once, when a severe flu epidemic nearly paralyzed Winder, I arrived home for dinner near 10 p.m., tired and irritable and feeling sorry for myself. Nora met me at the door, not with dinner, but with a list of three more house calls to make that night.

Disgustedly, I complained, "By the time these are finished, it will be 11 o'clock and the train should be coming through town. Maybe I should run in front of that train and let you get a husband who will stay at home with you sometimes."

Nora replied in her sweetest voice, "Honey, if you're going to do that, please take the old car."

When the last one of my four brothers experienced his heart attack, Nora heard me complain "Maybe I had better slow down."

Nora's response came with a twinkle in her eye, "If you slow down, you'll be backing up."

Her message came through loud and clear. *My chosen profession demanded my absolute best effort and much of my time.* It never failed to stop my feeling sorry for myself, and send me back to work.

In life, Nora encouraged me to gather my stories and listened patiently to many recitations of unusual and/or funny tales of experiences with patients, friends, neighbors and acquaintances. Now, after her death so unexpected and premature, I can almost hear her say in her own kind, loving way, "Go for it!"

So, Nora, here goes!

Acknowledgments

It would be impossible for me to name each person among the many patients, peers and friends who have encouraged me over many years to put these and other stories in print. Though I am grateful to each and every one for his/her encouragement, a simple general "Thank you" will have to suffice here.

To my stepson, Samuel Y (Sam) Morris, a genuine "Thank you" is given for his diligent work on the cover drawing, which is his original work. To Mrs. Harold Harrison, appreciation is noted for her financial help in publishing the book.

To my wife, Penny, my love and thanks for many editing suggestions. To Phil Hudgins, syndicated newspaper columnist, many thanks for proofreading and editing comments and for giving me proper credit and hyping this book as he retold some of my stories in his syndicated column.

Most of all, my heartfelt and sincere gratitude goes to my former newspaper editor, Myles Godfrey, who was first to publish any of my works, and who has been my encourager, advisor, mild critic, editor and friend through this and other literary endeavors. None of my written works would exist had he not believed in me and given an elderly, untrained, would-be-author a chance to be published as a columnist in his local newspaper, *The Barrow Eagle*. I shall be eternally grateful.

Contents

Dedication 7
Acknowledgments 9
Apology 15

Chapter 1   What Is This Older Generation Coming To? 19
    The Scenic Route 20
    The Man Upstairs 21
    Cause For A Cold 23
    Dirty Laundry 24
    Stamp It "Paid In Full" 26
    Use Your Own Bed 27
    How To Lose Weight Fast 28
    "Just Ain't Wuffa Damn" 29
    Feminine Power 30
    True Love Endures 31
    Wine Is A Mocker—Strong Drink Is Raging 32
    Buffet-Line Chatter 34

Chapter 2   Fon 35
    Driving A Wreck 36
    A Measurement Of His Wife? 36
    Bad Tasting Medicine 37

Chapter 3   Doctors Can Be Funny, Too 38
    Not A "Roll-Your-Own" 38
    A Sure Cure For Hiccups 40
    The Smoke Test 40
    Mamie 41
    Get An Answering Service 42
    Great Names For The Location 43

Not My End 44
The Real Purpose 45
Doctor Tom 47
A Promise Breaker 49
I Had Rather Shave 51
Perfect Planning? 51

Chapter 4   Sports And Sporting Stories 54

They're Coming To Take Me Away, Ha Ha! 55
I Want To Play 57
Zip 59
The Preacher's Story 59
Papa's Other Choice 60
Fishing With Doc 61
A Regular Stick-In-The-Mind 62
American Ingenuity 63
A Fisherman's Oxymoron 65

Chapter 5   Simply Picturesque Speech 66

All Inclusive Pain 67
Total Agony 67
How About Your Shadow? 67
These Cheap Time Pieces 67
The "Locked" Bowels 67
Drunk Again 67
That's A Digestive System 68
A Good Toothache? 68
Watch Those Grasshoppers 68
Papa Seems To Be Better 68
Miss Lannie 69
Beaten At My Own Game 69
Ophelia And Samantha 71
An Unlikely Cure 71
The Tense Test 72

Chapter 6   Functional Mispronunciations 74

    Proper Name For An Electrocardiogram 76
    Did You Say "Strep" Throat? 76
    Hiatal Hernia? 77
    Say No To Vertigo 77

Chapter 7   Just Funny Stories 79

    Triply Innocent 79
    Slide Carefully 81
    Enough Is Enough 82
    Getting Ready For Christmas 84
    How Was He To Know? 85
    Holler "Snake" 86
    Jack's Uncle Bill 88
    Welcome, Hot Flashes 90
    Who Is Putting Up With What? 90
    The Sheriff Of Clacktown 91
    Soft Drinks Cause This? 93

Chapter 8   Highs And Lows 95

    World Famous Teacher 96
    Jimson Weed Jumpies 98
    The Only Case 100
    Ecstasy And Agony 101
    Measles Manufactured Mayhem 105

Chapter 9   North Georgia Sweet Potato 107

    Beef Heart? 108
    Just A Starving Boy 108
    His Name Is "Tater" 110

Chapter 10   Oh! Those Kidney Stones! 111

    Testimony Of My Good Looks 112
    A Drink Out Of My Bottle 112
    Old Hammond 113

Chapter 11   The Titleholder 114
    No Time To Lie 115
    Two Windmills 116
    Camping Out 116
    A Trash-Moving Rain 117
    Sam Boon Goes Fishing With Me 118

Chapter 12   More Outlandish Tales 120
    The Original Purpose 120
    A Commercial Venture? 121
    Gretel And Tolbert 122
    Aunt Mable 123
    B-Bomb's Big Boo-Boo 125
    Another Crisis 126
    As High As You're Going 128
    The Wrong Man? 128
    Get Used It It, Pal 129
    Seen On TV 130
    Hawaii? 131
    An Unusual Bat 131
    Slow Poke 132

Chapter 13   Church-Related And/Or Spiritual Stories 133
    A Nation Of Look-Alikes 134
    Calling Assured 135
    Aunt Mable Keeps Her Appointment 138
    My Personal Parable 139
    Miss Rosa And The Deacons 142
    A Missionary At Heart 144

Chapter 14   Mattie 147

Apology

It may be presumptuous for me to think any reader would care how this book came to be written. However, this is my one chance to tell those to whom it may matter and, regardless of how presumptuous, my reasons for its writing are given now:

Although this is not my first attempt at composition, it is by far my boldest. My first attempt surfaced as a small, redheaded, freckle-faced, five-year old, who lived in the small town of Riverdale, Georgia. Even though it is now a thriving part of Metropolitan Atlanta, Riverdale, in those days, had only one small general store. My memory says it was called Munday's Store. The depression had our family firmly in its grip so no money existed for such luxuries as stick peppermint candy. That did not keep this redhead from dreaming as he pressed his snotty nose against Mr. Munday's candy counter. Out of that necessity, my first composition came into being.

It was a little song to be sprung upon anyone in the store who would listen. The words went like this:

> Charlie, he's a good little boy.
> Charlie, he's a dandy.
> Charlie, he's a good little boy.
> And he likes striped candy.

In those dark, depression days, not much candy rewarded that routine, but it served as the beginning of a cycle of composition.

Our wonderful English language has intrigued me and been the source of much pleasure throughout most of my lifetime. Any story with a play on words becomes my story, especially if the wordplay has a medical connotation. Memories are still fresh of the juvenile laughter evoked, at least in me, by the cajoling tease certain to be heard when a boy had a runny nose:

> "Johnny is plumb backwards. His nose is running and his feet are smelling."

In high school, great fortune brought me under the tutelage of Miss Lois Parr. Why we called such ladies "Miss" is a mystery to me because it seemed she never missed one thing I did incorrectly. Nevertheless, Miss Parr gained my attention and aroused in me a great appreciation of our language, to the point of having a love for it. Under her careful instruction, my appreciation of words and word-games grew markedly. I must thank her for raising in me a never-before-seen spark of literary enjoyment.

From high school, it was on to college at Mercer University. Here, my Professor of English, Dr. Herman Jones, stood in line to attempt to shape this young, unformed bit of rural clay. What a task he had! At 8:00 a.m., the clay seemed particularly rigid from sleepiness, not to mention all its other shortcomings of naivete, immaturity, and pure ignorance.

Well, Mercer had succeeded with "Sambo," (Dr. Ferrol Sams, author of *Run With The Horsemen*, and other books) and with Olive Ann (Olive Ann Burns, author of *Cold Sassy Tree*). Why not with me?

After completing college and still singularly unsuccessful as a writer, I had to heed the call of a dear Uncle who needed my presence to help him win a war.

How do you win a war as a Second Lieutenant Infantry assigned to a Grave Registration unit? Well, that's a story for another day.

Both the Germans and the Japanese apparently heard about my coming and simply threw in the towel before my training was complete. Obviously, they did not have the heart to face me.

But even two years in the Army produced no journalistic outflow from me except for a few vintage letters to girls, usually in distant ports of call. Let's hope these will never be published.

Having won the war, I headed back to school and an even harder job, that of winning the hand of my beloved Nora. Nevertheless, my pursuit of her continued until our lives flowed together, and we went off to Emory University to pursue our chosen careers—hers in nursing, and mine in medicine.

After all, Emory had succeeded with "Sambo." Why not with me?

While at Emory, I endured many tours of duty at Grady Memorial Hospital. At the time, the hospital was divided into two supposedly equal but separate units for whites and for blacks. Many people correctly referred to the two units as "The Gradies."

The memory of the first patient assigned to me at The Gradies remains indelible in my mind...an elderly black man with severe heart disease. My assignment loomed to record a complete history and do a physical examination on this old gentleman. My write-up would become a part of his permanent medical record, and thus be my first permanently recorded public writing. It began as a very trying experience, but this particular patient made it even more trying.

My patient had no formal education but, when I questioned, "What medicines are you taking?" he responded with names of several medications I easily recognized. Then he added in almost a postscript fashion, "And some dizzy tablets."

For three or four days, my every spare minute was spent trying to find what type of "dizzy tablets" he might be taking. Finally, his family members brought in his bottle of Digitalis, one of the oldest and most familiar medicines of all time.

Flabbergasted and feeling dumb, at that critical time my mind was impregnated with the journalistic tendency to hear well what a person says, then attempt to interpret what is really meant by their statements.

Since that time for a period of more than 50 years, I have gathered with pleasure from patients, friends, kinfolk, neighbors, and other associates some of the funniest and/ or most picturesque stories you can imagine. It seems to me it would be a shame for them to die simply because death, someday, will also close my mouth.

This is my effort to pass these stories on, thereby preserving them for posterity.

CHAPTER 1

WHAT IS THIS OLDER GENERATION COMING TO?

MUCH FUSS HAD BEEN made that "children say the darnedest things" and, without any question, they do. My experience is, however, their sayings do not by any manner of means outshine the things some of our senior citizens say (and do). In the ensuing pages, a few examples of hilarious senior incidents from my own experience and/or observation are reported.

The words chosen by some of these elder statesmen and ladies are often priceless. Are their funny remarks made with considerable forethought and malice, or are they spoken spontaneously in total innocence? More often than not, one is left to wonder which is the case and to ponder whether you have been taken in by some senior citizen's devious deception.

In my relatively long experience in the practice of medicine, just when I began to think every story and/or saying one could imagine had passed my way, I would be blindsided with a brand-new version that would cause my sides to split with laughter.

Over the years, my collection of great original stories has grown and I love to tell them. May I share them with you now?

The Scenic Route

Floogie had survived 93 hard years and her skin remained markedly wrinkled from age and the effects of many years of diligent, dutiful farm labor in southern sunshine. She and her family barely eked out a living from a Georgia-red-clay farm. Not one tooth existed in her head, a condition that worsened the facial wrinkle situation and gave her the appearance that even her wrinkles had wrinkles. The toothlessness also made her rounded chin become the most prominent part of her face as it jutted out strikingly below her gummy grin. In spite of advanced years and hard times, Floogie still had a great sense of humor.

She was a resident of one of the local nursing homes and sustained a fracture of her left hip when, one, night, she fell as she attempted to get out of bed. She was brought to our small emergency room, where it fell my lot to see her.

About two years before, Floogie had fractured her right hip in a similar fall. That previous fracture had been treated by surgery at one of the hospitals in Athens, Georgia. Now Athens is by no means a metropolis, but it does boast two fine hospitals: the community hospital, Athens Regional Medical Center, and the Catholic Hospital, St. Mary's.

At the time, our hospital had no one on its staff who was qualified to do reconstructive hip surgery. There remained no choice for me but to again refer Floogie to Athens for her orthopedic procedure.

"Which hospital would you want me to call for you?" I queried my elderly patient.

"Hit don't differ…air one," came her reply.

"Would you like to be sent to the same hospital where you had surgery before?" my questioning continued.

"At 'ud be raeel niice," she responded in her most agreeable tone of voice.

Not being able to remember which of the two hospitals had been chosen in the past, my inquiry pressed on, "Well, Floogie, which hospital were you in before?"

She answered my question with a question of her own: "Do you know 'at 'air one whut's got all of them Catholic Mothers and Sisters at it?"

"Yes, I do," I replied, as in my mind I was already calling Saint Mary's Hospital.

"Well, they had me at the t'other 'un," replied Floodie.

In my opinion, she took the scenic route to inform me of her prior admission to Athens Regional Medical Center.

THE MAN UPSTAIRS

Miss Ocie had taught school for more than 50 years, having continued her teaching career well beyond normal retirement age. She always taught children in the primary grades, never above the third grade level. She made a practice of sitting as she taught and, when she went home, she continued to sit a majority of the time because her sister, Miss Marie, did most of the housework. As a result of so many sitting years with little physical activity, Miss Ocie developed quite a large backside and extremely puny arm muscles.

One night while attending a PTA meeting, Miss Ocie fell. Her complaint of severe hip pain caused her to be brought to the emergency room where I became her physician. X-rays showed a displaced fracture of the femoral neck in her left hip. Doctor Stone, an orthopedic surgeon from Athens, was consulted and made the 20 mile drive to Winder.

Dr. Stone decided to do her surgery in the local hospital where Miss Ocie could be closer to relatives and friends. Here, they could visit her more easily and be of greater assistance in her rehabilitation. After admission to a second-story room in our two-story hospital, her surgery was done without complication and Miss Ocie was returned to her room for rehabilitation.

Physiotherapy remained in its infancy in those days, with the closest physiotherapy department just being formed at Emory University. Metal walkers had not yet made their appearance in the common marketplace. This made rehabilitation much more difficult than it is today, because we could offer nothing more than crutches to Miss Ocie to help her walk again.

She had a great problem trying to handle her large backside using only crutches. Her puny arm muscles and lack of agility made it nearly an impossibility. Dr. Stone and I put her on a daily regimen of lifting small dumbbells to strengthen her arm muscles and increase her coordination, really an innovative therapy for that era in medicine.

Days of little or no progress towards Miss Ocie's ambulation turned into weeks. In my opinion, she seemed to not be working very hard with her muscle-building exercises, and my impatience heightened with each passing day. Weeks of no progress turned into a month. As we were about to begin the second month in which she had not taken one single step, the fact appeared obvious that some type of action must be taken now, and it was my duty to take it.

One Sunday morning, I walked into her room and made my stern statement, "Miss Ocie, the doctors and nurses have done what we can do for you. Your hip is nailed in exceptionally good position and x-rays show healing is taking place.

"Two months have passed, and you have not taken even one step. You do not seem to be working hard at the exercises we devised for you and are not gaining the strength we had expected."

My spiel continued, "I cannot walk for you. The nurses cannot walk for you. In fact, whether or not you ever take another step is strictly between you and "The Man Upstairs!"

Having said my piece, I whirled and left the room, not waiting for a reply.

Miss Ocie turned to Miss Marie and blustered, "I thought we were on the top floor."

[Author's Note:] Indeed Miss Ocie did walk again, due in large measure to her family. They found for her the first walker I had ever seen; a cumbersome, heavy-steel, three-sided, cage-like contraption on rollers. A canvass back-strap and a seat that could be raised and lowered formed the fourth side, and served as a gate. Welded to the top rail on each side were steel equivalents of the arm-pieces of crutches.

Cumbersome as it appeared, it became an answer to prayer, Miss Ocie could be allowed to stand at her bedside while an attendant backed up the walker and closed it around her. She could then lean on the walker rails to walk, or sit safely on the seat if she lost her balance or got tired. She felt secure in using this modern marvel and worked quite hard toward rehabilitation.

In the ensuing years, she and Miss Marie took many strolls over Barrow County's rolling hills. Despite my stern lecture, she and I remained close friends until her death and we laughed many times about the incident of "The Man Upstairs."

Cause For A Cold

Lawrence, a grinning, mischievous, happy-go-lucky, rotund kid of about 70 years appeared to be the kind of fellow who could, and would, have fun at a funeral. Even when he became very ill, he never lost his sense of humor. He came into the office one day with an obviously really bad cold.

"Lawrence," I asked, "how did you ever manage to catch such a terrible cold?"

Lawrence grinned as he made his quick and to-the-point reply. "Well, Doc, I really don't know for certain how I got it, but I think it might be because of these cool nights we've been a'havin' here lately. You know how cold it's been a'gettin' every night these past few weeks, especially early in the mornin'. Well, all that time, I ain't been sleeping under nothing but one thin woman."

One has to admit Lawrence may have had a point here. "Under" exposure could possibly bring just as much harm as we have been warned lies in overexposure.

Dirty Laundry

Mrs. Sosebee and her family had been my patients for several years. She had been diagnosed as suffering from an obsessive-compulsive personality disorder with a fixation on extreme cleanliness. This obsession caused her to sometimes wash her hands more than 200 times a day, and often required treatment for a skin disorder brought on by the excessive hand-washing.

On this particular visit to my office, Mrs. Sosebee's massively swollen, red and feverish right leg loomed as the problem. Moderate tenderness was demonstrated in the calf and her body temperature showed a mild elevation. The dreaded Homan's sign tested positive, meaning she experienced pain in the calf as you flexed the toes upward with a little force.

Beyond any doubt, she had a severe case of acute thrombophlebitis—inflammation and clots in the veins—in that leg. To prevent those blood clots from moving to her lungs, possibly with dire consequences, including death, she needed immediate hospitalization for bed rest with intensive anticoagulation and antibiotic therapy.

"This is a dangerous situation and we are going to have to admit you immediately to the hospital for treatment," I explained as I began to write hospital admission orders.

"No! I am not going to any hospital!" responded Mrs. Sosebee sternly. "You will just have to find some way to treat me at home," she added with equal emphasis.

The defiant stand taken by this usually mild-mannered patient revealed a side of her that surprised me greatly.

"But," I pleaded my case with her, "you might have a blood clot break off and go to your lungs. It could possibly kill you instantly.

Dirty Laundry Don't Take No Doctor's Orders

You need intense hospital treatment for this condition. Your life could very well depend on it!"

Mrs. Sosebee refused with a resounding "No! No! No!" There was no reason to speak further. She refused…"absolutely!"

"Okay," I responded in submission, "since you choose to refuse my advice to go to the hospital, you cannot ask me to bear any responsibility if a blood clot goes to your lungs and kills you. That is your choice and you will have to bear all responsibility for any consequences of it. I will need you to sign a statement to that effect and we will have it put into your medical record."

Mrs. Sosebee readily signed the statement releasing me from responsibility of consequences for her actions.

"I will try to treat you at home," I submitted, "but you must stay in the bed; and I mean *in the bed* to the extent you have all your meals brought to the bed and use a pot at your bedside. Use the remote control for the TV or get someone else to change the channels for you.

"Keep your leg elevated on three pillows at all times with a heating pad wrapped around the calf, but be careful not to burn your leg. Get this prescription filled and take the pills exactly as I directed. I will see you in the office this coming Tuesday if you don't have to come to the emergency room before that date. If you go to the emergency room, take these orders I have written, but I wish you would change your mind and go to the hospital right now."

"Thank you, but no," Mrs. Sosebee said resolutely, as she took her prescription, hospital orders and return appointment. She left the office with her husband who, after shrugging his shoulders to indicate his helplessness or unwillingness to influence her, had remained absolutely silent during my entire conversation with his wife.

The following Tuesday when Mr. Sosebee dutifully showed up in my office at the appointed time, it seemed perfectly obvious she had not been in bed. Her leg appeared more swollen than before and the redness and heat had increased. My unhappiness with the entire situation obviously showed.

I began to tell her of my displeasure until Mrs. Sosebee gently patted my arm to interrupt me. She explained in the gentlest, softest, sweetest voice, "But, Doctor Skelton, surely you are smart enough to know that dirty laundry don't take no doctor's orders!"

Her logic overwhelmed me. This lady considered cleanliness the most important thing in the world…even worth the risk of death. Her treatment continued at home, because she still gave me no other option.

Mrs. Sosebee got well with no further problems and no permanent damage that we could recognize.

What do we doctors know?

Stamp It "Paid In Full"

Addiezue had been my friend and patient for many years. Not a frequent visitor to my office by any measure, it was a sure bet something was wrong when she did darken my door. Together, we had already fought the battles of heart disease and pneumonia and even went through a scare of possible tuberculosis. This time, it appeared to be cancer of the tongue, and it called for radical surgery immediately.

The surgery required removal of half her tongue, part of her lower jaw and a radical dissection of all lymph nodes in the left side of her neck. Despite all adversities, Addiezue remained as good a soldier in these trying times as she had always been. Her keen sense of humor persisted even as she had to learn to speak again.

About this time, my wife gave birth to our fifth child—the fifth daughter. My boast had always been we would either have a boy, or would fill the woods with little girls. When Nora informed me in no uncertain terms the woods were filled with girls, I had to submit because of her health problems.

Addiezue heard the news of our fifth daughter and phoned me. With great difficulty in her speaking, and equal difficulty in my understanding, she informed me, "Yeah, de Debbil owe you a debt, an' is gonna pay it in son-in-laws."

Addiezue hit the nail on the head, but you can now stamp that debt, "Paid in full."

Use Your Own Bed

The elderly couple's oldest daughter called and begged me to come see her mother, who had never been my patient. Pneumonia loomed high on my list of suspicions because the daughter told me she had a high fever and a cough. We agreed I would make a house call as soon as my own office patients had been seen.

Much to the chagrin of her husband, the old lady's regular doctor vacationed out of town and would not be back for several days. The old man really had rather they had waited for *the* doctor to return. My being relatively new in the community and having never before seen his wife seemed to be extremely disconcerting to him and he had several questions to ask. Suffice it to say, he was not overjoyed by my presence and let his feelings be known.

Fully aware of his total lack of confidence, I offered to leave. However, the rest of the family were unanimous in their opinion. Mama was too ill to wait for her regular doctor. Although I felt uneasy about the situation, the family prevailed on me to stay.

The walls of the old house where they lived had never been painted and were darkened by smoke from many years of fireplace heating. High nonreflecting ceilings made my task more difficult, with the only light source being from the 40-watt bulb dangling on a cord in the middle of the room. As my examination took place, I had a feeling of claustrophobia brought on by the darkness of the room and the hovering of the above-80-year-old husband and two daughters.

The low bed in which the old lady slept bridged only slightly above the floor and made it a difficult stretch to bend over and reach her for examination. I could not help but think, *there is no way they could have a slopjar under this bed.* When time came to examine her lungs, she complied with my request to sit upright for examination of the back of her chest but, on that low bed even with her in an upright position, it still produced a back strain to bend and reach around to the back of her chest with my stethoscope.

Therefore, I sat behind her on the bed to examine her lungs, thinking nothing of this action because it had always been my procedure and the practice of my teachers in medical school. Sounds of pneumonia were clearly present.

To my chagrin and surprise, the loudest sounds I heard were of an irate old man saying, "Humph! I've been married to that woman for more than 60 years, and that's the first time I've ever seen another man in bed with her!

With the treatment I gave her, the old lady got well, but they never called me to their house again nor did I have the slightest desire to be called.

Although my external reaction was laughter, my ego suffered greatly. I mused in self-defense as I tried to place the experience behind me: there is no way you can win them all—and, besides, you never thought you could treat the whole world.

How To Lose Weight Fast

One of the earliest canned liquid meals for weight loss was called Sego. The product design called for a can of Sego to take the place of a meal, since it contained enough calories and nutrients to be a complete meal. Sego enjoyed extensive use in this area where our staple diets were very high in carbohydrates and fats and caused us to have a lot of obese folks.

One of the main reasons for its popularity in this area, I believe, could be traced to the recommendation by Miss Evelyn, the fabulous wife of one of Barrow County's most prominent older physicians. She would laughingly say, "It really is good. Especially when you put a big scoop of ice cream in it!"

At the height of Sego's popularity, a fairly old couple came under my care for high blood pressure and diabetes, complicated by being grossly overweight. As fate would have it, the couple operated a cafe that catered to meals for plant and mill workers. They featured plate-meals piled high with starchy foods and vegetables that would stick to a man's ribs and give him energy to perform hard labor.

In that kind of environment, it seemed difficult for this couple to lose weight needed for control of their other ailments. In spite of the odds, we continued to make an attempt.

They were seen frequently in my office and were given blood pressure medications considered proper in that day and time. Again and again, they were encouraged to lose weight.

Every visit to the office scales became a scene of disappointment. They appeared to be genuinely dumbfounded by their failure to control their weight, as hard as they were trying. Even though both of them claimed to be religiously adhering to the prescribed diet, they showed no evidence of results.

I walked into their cafe one day at the time of the noonday meal, and saw both of my patients sitting at the lunch counter. Two special plant-workers plates were in front of them, piled high with food. I then joined them in wondering why they could not lose weight since each of them was dutifully drinking a can of Sego… with their meal.

What more could they do?

"Just Ain't Wuffa Damn"

Mr. Asbury claimed to be 85 years old, but remained active as a farmer. He appeared robust and healthy despite his age. Most of his kinfolk claimed to be devout Christians, although some seemed to be anything but Christians, I did not know the status of Mr. Asbury's faith.

Mr. Asbury did not cotton much to doctors and he certainly did not cotton to spending one red cent that was not an absolute necessity. He was not cheap. That was just the way it had to be if you raised 13 children on a southern farm during the depression and post-depression era.

Assuming his devoutness and knowing of his forced frugality, I felt certain it was a true emergency when our emergency room requested me to see Mr. Asbury on a Sunday morning. Therefore, I skipped church and went to check him.

"Mr. Asbury," I inquired, "what is your problem?"

"Well, Doctor," he snorted, "I just ain't wuffa damn."

"What do you mean by 'ain't wuffa damn?'" I questioned.

His submissive reply came, "Doctor, I can follow my old mule all right all morning long but come dinnertime, I just can't follow him home to save my life."

My hat tipped to Mr. Asbury, acknowledging him as a better man this this doctor would ever be. Sadly, no treatment existed at that time to slow the real cause of his problem, advancing hardening of the arteries. A couple of years later, a stroke would cost him his life.

Feminine Power

"A few weeks after Tap and I got married," Grace recalled, "I got so homesick I thought I would die, so I jumped in my car and drove home. When I got there, my parents were in their A-model Ford, ready to go to protracted meeting," (as Church Revivals were often called at the time).

"Man, I felt so homesick," Grace continued, "I would have done anything to see Mama and Papa, so I just piled in the back seat of that A-model and went with them. When we got there, the preacher, Rev. Grotus McSweet, spoke on 'Marriage and the Home'".

"During the course of his message, Rev. McSweet said, 'I can truthfully say that in all our years of marriage, me and my wife have never spoken one cross word,'" Grace's soliloquy continued.

"After church, we were riding home and Mama turned to Papa and confessed, "Tom, I don't believe what Grotus said tonight.'

"About whut?' Papa replied.

"About they ain't never said one cross word," Mama answered.

"Doctor Skelton, you know my Papa wasn't one to talk against anybody," Grace said, smiling and turning aside. "It seemed he would never reply to Mama, as he steered that car and thought. When he finally spoke, his words were, 'Well,…I don't know. He could be right. But I'll bet there were some powerful poutin' spells around that house!'"

True Love Endures

Belma sounded badly worried when she called about her neighbor. "She has been sick for two days with nausea and vomiting and has been talking out of her head," she explained.

"Yes, she's too sick to come to the office and, besides, we ain't got no way to bring her," came Belma's reply to my next obvious question.

"Yes, I know she's not your patient but I just can't stand to see the pore thing suffer," she answered my objection. We agreed on a house-call as soon as my workload would allow, knowing it would be late at night.

After about a 12 mile drive, my arrival at the "pore thing's" house came, indeed, late at night. Everything appeared absolutely dark and the house seemed tightly shut. The family had obviously already gone to bed. My concern for the patient's health and my time investment told me, *It's too late to turn back now.* I knocked loudly on the door.

After a short wait, I heard a stirring of someone coming to open the door. Then, louder noises ensued as the responder fell to the floor—not once or twice—but three times before he opened the door and let me enter. Cloyd was obviously drunk.

On entering the house, I saw my patient lying on a bed near the door, but she did not pay me one bit of attention. Instead, she spoke angrily and loudly to her husband, "Cloyd, you got me drunk and stole my gummint check." (In Southernese, that's government check.)

"Yes, you did! Then you reached in my pillow case and stole my check so you could buy likker. Cloyd, you SOB," (except she did not use initials) "if I didn't love you, I would beat your ass until it wouldn't hold corn shucks."

After hearing this exchange, it did not take a genius to figure why she was "talking out of her head." My patient had what we often referred to as "Ball-Mason flu," a common term used among people in surrounding counties to describe being drunk. Its name derived because moonshine whiskey, a frequent cause for it, usually came in fruit jars, and the most common brand of jars were "Ball-Mason." I had seen many a man suffer from this flu but, in those days, to see a woman so afflicted seemed much more rare.

Her serious threat to Cloyd, coupled with such an ardent expression of love, gave me cause to ponder. With Cloyd in that condition, she might carry out the threat right there in my presence. If she could only get out of bed.

Later, Cloyd's wife developed cancer, she became a regular patient. Because of this cancer, she became quite emaciated and my partner admitted her to the hospital to build up her strength and weight. One day, when Dr. Graves went into her room she exclaimed excitedly, "Doctor, I think it's working. I'm puttin' on a little weight. See," she gleefully pointed to her lower abdomen, "I've got a little pot-gut. Of course, it ain't much bigger than a teacup."

And her description proved accurate.

Wine Is A Mocker—Strong Drink Is Raging

(Proverbs 20: 1)

His liver, virtually destroyed by cirrhosis, seemed moderately tender and felt stony hard. One could easily feel it below his rib margin, a sure sign it had become swollen, probably during his last heavy bout with his only friend—his bottle of liquor. The whites of his eyes were pumpkin yellow from jaundice, a symptom he had experienced many times before.

He looked feeble and emaciated, yet he showed no desire to eat adequately. At first, we thought he would die either from the effects of his cirrhosis or from the DT's which often racked his frail body despite our best efforts to control the frenzied convulsions.

Slowly—oh, so slowly—he began to respond to the treatment, and then, as he had done many times before, he rapidly improved until the time came for him to be discharged from the hospital.

One of the unsettling difficulties in his case remained that he lived in Atlanta, a long distance from my office, and could be seen only when one of his family members found him at home too weak from drinking to resist their efforts to bring him to the hospital for treatment.

Deeming it my duty, I began to instruct him about his care at home and especially of the need to stay away from Demon Rum. I had given the same advice to innumerable patients, including several times to him. At the request of his family, I laid it on extra thick this time, stressing the fact that HE was the one who would have to make a change if he wanted to continue to live.

"Your liver is so badly damaged, I do not believe you could possibly survive another episode of drinking like this one," I said in an opening statement designed to be dramatic. "You were so sick, we thought for certain you would die on this admission."

"Most of your problem is caused by alcohol and you simply must stop drinking if you want to live. It's a matter of life and death for you and it's a thing you must do for yourself. No one else can do it for you," continued my pleading.

"I can't *not* drink for you!" I exclaimed in dramatic fashion, hoping it would be the coup de gras.

He caught me by the hand and, with a wink, twinkle in his eye and a wry smile on his face, interrupted this old tee-totaling

Southern Baptist with, "I'll tell you what, Doctor. You do my *not* drinking for me and I'll do your drinking for you!"

Oh well, I preached a good sermon and there have been converts with it before and since, but this just seemed not to be my day to convert this particular old sot. I never saw him after that nor did I hear from him again, which made me think my prophecy of his death may well have been self-fulfilling.

Buffet-Line Chatter

Susie, the daughter of a locally prominent lawyer, was a doted-on, only child who seemed surprisingly sweet and unspoiled. Each member of her family had been my patients in recent years.

Susie's wedding had been held on Saturday, and she had done me the honor of requesting that I sing. The affair proved to be a high social event for our community, attended by many prominent people of Barrow and surrounding counties. It went without a hitch, except for the usual intended hitching done by a marriage ceremony.

On Sunday after the wedding, many Barrow Countians gathered for the open-to-the-public buffet served weekly at the Elks Club Dining Room, and attended by many of the more affluent members of the community. It became a great place to keep up with the news, and the good food seemed relatively inexpensive.

Ms. Sylvia, the mentally declining matron of one of the more influential families in our area, having lawyers, judges and governors in her direct lineage, stood ahead of me in the serving line. "Dr. Skelton," she remarked, "you surely did sing sweet at Susie's funeral."

Having shocked me with that misstatement, she licked the serving spoon, and replaced it in the casserole.

I chose the spoon on the far side of the dish for my serving.

CHAPTER 2

Fon

F<small>ON REIGNED AS HEAD</small> *of his clan—the patriarch, if you please. He had lived to a ripe old age despite his impropriety with local moonshine whiskey, and his dangerous occupation of sawmilling. Over his lifetime, Fon had collected many interesting stories both real and imagined. He enjoyed telling and retelling these whenever the family or anyone else gathered, and had gotten to be rather good at it. One had best soon learn, however, that if you took Fon's stories seriously, you did it at your own risk.*

Because Fon's mouth proved not to be exactly a prayer book, people in this area felt you had to watch him closely in business dealings. No one ever reported him to actually cheat anybody, but he had been known to stretch the truth a little at times.

Fon had an old Model A Ford he wanted to sell, and I desired just as eagerly to buy it. However, a car such as his had no certificate of title to be transferred. Having heard that one should take care in business dealings with him, I wanted a witness to our transaction. We were on our way to the Barrow County Sheriff's office for that purpose when Fon shared this story with me:

Driving a Wreck

"You know, Doctor," said Fon, "a while back, me an' my wife had a car accident, an' we wuz both hurt pretty bad. We both stayed in the horspital fer a while, but she wuz hurt worser'n I wuz an' she stayed in the horspital longer'n I did.

"I come up town here an' I run into Orscum Haddix. You know him. He's the one what founded the Persons Bank here. Of course you know him. Shucks, he's still the President and Chairman of the board of that thing.

"Anyhow, Mister Orscum says to me, he says, 'Fon what's this I hear 'bout you a'havin' a accident? Shucks, there ain't no sense in that. Now me, I been a'drivin' a car for more'n 40 years, an' I ain't never had no wreck!'"

"Well, sir, I looked at him sorta quizzical like an' I says right back to him, 'You know, Mister Orscum, you'n me, we're sorta alike. Yet we're sorta differ'nt, too. Now me, I been a'drivin' a *wreck* fer more'n 40 years, an' I ain't never had no *car!*'"

I could vouch for the accuracy of Fon's assessment of his vehicles on the bais of personal observation.

A Measurement of His Wife?

My mental picture is still clear of Fon with his sparse, white hair and wrinkled, weather-worn face, grinning his almost toothless grin as he placed a pint fruit-jar on the receptionist's desk at my office. The jar was partially filled with a clear, yellowish liquid appearing to be of the same general type that one of my patients had aptly referred to as "toilet water" when she brought her own specimen for examination.

"Here's my wife's specification," drawled Fon. "The doctor tole me he had to check one before he could figger out what the heck is wrong with her. I ain't got time to wait now. I'll come back fer a report in the mornin', since we ain't got no telephone."

Without another word, he turned and left the room.

No blueprints, no measurements, nor any of the other things usually referred to as "specifications" were in the fruit-jar Fon left behind. I suppose it will always give me cause to wonder if he was just pulling my leg, or if he truly had problems with pronouncing the commonly used word "specimen."

Bad Tasting Medicine

"A number of years ago, my oldest boy got sick an' I taken him to see Dr. W. C. Bailen in Hoschton," Fon reported with a grin. "Doc give me some medicine fer him an' when I got home, I could not git that youngun to take that stuff no matter what I done.

"I done everything I knowed to do. I even taken a ole razor strop an' laid it hard on that youngun's behind, an I still couldn't git him to take it. So the next day," Fon continued, "I went back to that doctor's office and tole him, 'Doctor W. C., you're gonna have to give me some differ'nt medicine fer my boy, I reckon'.

"An' Doctor W.C. asked, 'Why's that, Fon?'

"An' I said, 'Cause I can't git him to take the stuff whut you give him yesterday.'

"An' Doctor W. C. asked again, 'Why's that, Fon?'

"An' I said, 'I reckon 'cause it don't taste good,'

"Then Doctor W. C. tole me, 'Fon, if you just want me to give him something that tastes good, I'll give him some candy.'"

It sounds reasonable to me.

CHAPTER 3

Doctors Can Be Funny, Too

Most people are absolutely convinced doctors are a bunch of stuffed-shirts who live in a sterile world and face life and death decisions every minute of the day. The gospel truth is, most doctors are human beings who face the same trials and tribulations as others. They also find themselves in the same type of funny situations in which other human beings are involved.

The following pages contain a few examples of some of the funny happenings to physicians, most of them witnessed by or happening to me... these things are rarely shared by men and women in my profession for fear our patients might see more of our imperfections, thereby putting further tarnish on our corporate halo.

Laugh with me now as we apply a little tarnish to our halo and image:

Not A "Roll-Your-Own"

My internship occurred before the great revelations about the many medical dangers of smoking. Most doctors who were in training at the time had just returned from active duty in the armed forces where virtually everyone smoked. Therefore, most physicians-in-training were smokers, as were most private physicians. Doctor Oschner in New Orleans had just begun to sound the alarm about an association between smoking and cancer of the lung but, since most of us were already addicted, we did not wish to listen to his "nonsense."

The hospital where I served my internship had a severe shortage of recruits for the year and an intern had to work seven days a week. His schedule called for 35 hours on and 13 hours off. He did get a two-weeks vacation with full pay but what paltry pay—a puny 20 dollars a month. Little money remained even for what were considered absolute necessities, things such as cigarettes.

Most of us were too poor and/or too tired to care about maintaining the social graces and amenities We were constantly bumming cigarettes from our peers. That deplorable situation brought about an unforgettable conversation between my friend, D. T., and a surgery resident from Arkansas named Hunter.

Walking down the hallway with the surgery resident, D. T. requested, "Hey, Hunter, give me a weed."

Hunter replied in his best Arkansas drawl, "Boy, you are a doctor and are supposed to be educated and dignified and refined. You ought not to just say 'Hey, Hunter, give me a weed.' You should say something in keeping with your profession—yes, something educated, dignified and refined—like, 'Pardon me, but could I be so bold as to trouble you for a ready-roll?'

"And, being a doctor," Hunter continued, "and being educated and dignified and refined, I would not just tell you, 'Hell no!' I would tell you something in keeping with my profession—yes, something educated and dignified and refined—like:

"Your eyes may shine and your teeth may grit. But if you think you're going to get one of my ready-rolls, you're full of it."

By this time, an amazed and amused D.T. began walking away from the group, already smoking the "ready-roll" given to him and lit by the laughing surgery resident from Arkansas.

A Sure Cure For Hiccups

Dr. Copeland, a third-year surgery resident, perspired profusely as he toiled in the operating room completely absorbed in the difficult task of removing a greatly infected gallbladder. The tense situation sustained an interruption when Dr. Heard, a first-year medical resident, entered the operating room. He wanted to discuss a different patient from the one on the operating table, yet one being treated by both doctors, who had been hiccupping without relief for six days.

Dr. Heard asked, "What more can we possibly do for our patient with hiccups? We have had him hold his breath for as long as possible, re-breathe in a paper bag for hours on end, frightened him with all kinds of loud noises, given him Phenergan by hypo and by mouth until I am afraid to give anymore, and done almost every other crazy thing anyone has suggested?"

Dr. Copeland, extremely upset by this intrusion at a time when he could not give it more intensive thought, made his flippant reply, "Stick an ice-cube up his rectum!"

Dr. Copeland continued his delicate surgery as Dr. Heard returned to the hospital ward. To the surprise of Dr. Copeland and all of the nursing staff on the ward, Dr. Heard did exactly as he had been instructed. To their even greater surprise, the patient's hiccups completely disappeared and did not return.

Do you suppose he was afraid to hiccup?

The Smoke Test

Dr. Copeland showed great excitement about one of his patients who had been proved to have an extremely rare condition called "gastro-colic fistula," an abnormal connection between the stomach and the large intestine. In this instance, the probem had been caused by an old stab wound to the abdomen where both organs had been penetrated and grew together in the scar tissue.

In his extensive reading about gastro-colic fistula, Dr. Copeland found an article in the very old medical literature, written before x-ray became available to help in diagnosis. The article suggested the diagnosis could be confirmed by blowing smoke in large quantities into the rectum of the patient suspected of having the condition. If the patient emitted smoke when he belched, the diagnosis stood confirmed. He reported to the medical staff on his literature search and included this article.

Not amused by our loud laughter in response to his report, Dr. Copeland promised, "Since you think it's so funny, I will just take this patient to the procto room and see if it works,"

In the proctoscopic room, he filled three large, heavy-duty balloons with cigar smoke and attached each to the inserted proctoscope until each balloon deflated. Within a few minutes, the gas-filled patient belched and coughed—of all things—cigar smoke.

The doctor's final report concluded, "The only failure of the test came when the patient could not identify what brand of cigar I used."

Mamie

Mamie, a petite, pretty, unmarried, fun-loving, black-haired RN with dancing black eyes proved to be an excellent nurse, and I truly enjoyed working with her. At that moment, my wife stood far advanced in her first pregnancy and being unfaithful to Nora did not enter my mind as I worked with Mamie.

Many mornings when we arrived at work, I would put my hand on Mamie's shoulder and say, "Mamie, you are feeling quite well this morning."

That routine soon got old and, to vary it, I placed my hand on her shoulder one day and remarked, "Mamie, you're not feeling very well this morning."

Mamie looked up at me with an extra sparkle in her dancing black eyes and replied, "Humph, big boy, maybe you're not feeling in the right places!"

It took a while to remove the red glow from my face and, after it faded, that routine would certainly never be tried again with Mamie. Perhaps, I had not been feeling in the right places, but Mamie certainly put me in my place.

Get An Answering Service

An acute shortage of doctors in our town led me to contact a young resident physician in Atlanta to encourage location of his medical practice here. He appeared clearly interested and visited Winder to check out the opportunity. While being shown all the attractions of our small town and its hospital, he met all of our physicians except for one of our senior physicians.

As we visited the home of this older doctor, he began to tell our possible recruit about the trials of family practice. "It is a trying profession and your time is not your own," he complained. "It is rare for me to sit down to a meal without having to get up to answer the phone or go to the door. We rarely have company in our home because I may have to leave.

"I can't even go to the bathroom without being interrupted! A compete night of sleep is something to dream about. In fact," he added, "my wife and I have seven children and I had to take her out of town seven times to get her pregnant."

Oh what a difficult life!

In spite of the warning, our recruit came to town and had several years of successful practice before leaving as a far wiser physician to impart some of his knowledge to medical students. Perhaps Doctor Alec's sad story is one of the reasons they now teach students in medical school, "Get an answering service!"

Great Names For The Location

My arrival in Winder as a bright-eyed, eager, young physician, certain he could take the world by storm, came without fanfare. Not knowing anyone to call on for help, I began in solo practice doing general medicine, pediatrics, obstetrics, surgery, orthopedics, and anything else that might come along. In a small-town general practice at that time, you had to be willing to work all hours of the day and/or night, seven days a week and you had to be willing to attempt anything and everything.

My acceptance did not occur immediately because another new physician had come to Winder just two weeks before my arrival. He grew up in Barrow County, so any person thinking about using a new doctor would naturally try the hometown boy first.

The average citizen described me as "that young fellow who doesn't look like a doctor, but more like a football player." To make matters even worse, a high percentage of residents in Barrow County repeatedly mispronounced my name, calling me "Dr. Skeleton" almost as often as they said "Dr. Skelton."

Gradually, by my taking anyone as a patient and going anywhere at any time, my practice began to increase. After a couple of years, my presence in the county had become fairly well-known, but the constant grind began to take its toll on both my mind and body.

Then, the unexpected happened. Two of our local physicians were called into the armed forces for the Korean conflict and my practice increased so dramatically, some help was needed immediately.

As fate would have it, another young doctor, Dr. Richard Forrest Graves, came to town about a year after my arrival. The two of us got along well from the beginning, and began to share calls. It seemed really wonderful to have an occasional break and become part of the family again.

After a year or so, we decided to buy an old building in town and convert it into professional offices. A young dentist joined us in the new venture. As we considered the remodeling of the building, it appeared our remodeling and our practices would be more efficient and cost effective if doctor Graves and I merged those practices and became full partners.

Both of our wives expressed fear of a partnership because it had never been done before in Winder. In spite of their stern warnings, we merged our practices and everything worked wonderfully. Our patients were happy because they knew a doctor would be available at all times and, when we were both there, they could take their choice. Expenses were cut and both practices grew substantially.

It just so happened that the building we remodeled had been used in the past as a funeral home. It stands as a testimony to our ability as physicians and our willingness to give good service, that our partnership succeeded even though it became a standing joke in town, "Doctors Skeleton and Graves are practicing in the old funeral home."

Not My End

She was well over 40, which is old for a first pregnancy. Adding to our problems, she had diabetes, obesity and both high blood pressure and kidney trouble. With all these complicating factors, as she got into the later stages of pregnancy, she developed problems. Cesarean section appeared to be in order and my friend, Dr. Monroe, agreed to assist me with the surgery.

Things went well and we delivered a huge, live baby girl with little difficulty. The mother had no serious problems after surgery, and left the hospital at the routine time. Because of minor wound drainage, we did not remove the sutures until a later office visit and, by this time, she had accumulated a small amount of pus around her lower stitches…not an unusual or frightening occurrence.

The father, Shifty, a hunchbacked person with congenital palsy, was noted for his surly disposition. Most people thought he came a few neurons short of being a simpleton, and many people, had problems getting along with him. He and I rarely had any such problems unless I spoke to him about his medical bill. My strategy evolved to never be too serious about anything with Shifty but to tease about almost everything. It seemed to be the easiest way to get along with him.

When he brought the Mrs. to the office for removal of her stitches, Shifty asked me, "How come the top part of her incision looks so good and the bottom part has got all that pus in it?"

Thinking he would know I was joking, I teased in return, "Oh, that's the end Dr. Monroe sewed up."

For the next few weeks, Dr. Monroe showed marked coolness toward me. In fact, he even deliberately went out of his way to avoid me. Not being one who has enough friends to give up one without trying to do something about it, I cornered Dr. Monroe in the doctor's lounge and asked him about the problem between us.

His answer genuinely shocked me, though in retrospect it should not have. Shift had gone to Dr. Monroe's office and made a loud and embarrassing scene in the waiting room.

He demanded loudly, "How come the end of my wife's cut Doctor Skelton sewed up looks so good and the one you sewed up has got old pus in it? I'll tell you one thing right now, I ain't a'gonna pay you 'til it heals." (He failed to tell Dr. Monroe he would never pay me.)

Naturally, Dr. Monroe became angry and I did not blame him, but, after we talked it out, we remained good friends. When Dr. Monroe later completed a residency and moved to a neighboring town as a surgeon, I reminded him many times this story did not become funny to him until he grew to be a big-time specialist who wanted me to send those referrals.

The Real Purpose

A large reception celebrated Dr. Monroe's completion of his surgical residency and entering into a surgical partnership. The reception, held in the magnificent home of his new partner, featured live Maine lobster flown in from New England to be the fare of the evening. The party proved elegant, supervised in a charming way by the beautiful, poised wife of Dr. Monroe's new associate. Every aspect of the evening seemed to be perfect.

As the evening neared a close, a receiving line of hosts and their wives assembled to bid their guests goodnight. Nora and I retrieved our coats and entered the line to say our good-byes.

"Red and Nora," remarked Dr. Monroe's associate, "we are so glad you could come. We have valued your friendship over the years and really do hope you will come back to see us real soon. By the way, Red, I have some surgery scheduled in Winder next Thursday, I'll see you then, if you're around the hospital."

We thanked him for the invitation and stated how much we had enjoyed the evening.

Next in line came our charming hostess who exclaimed in her seemingly sincere and gracious way, "Oh, Nora, Doctor Skelton, we are so delighted you graced us with your presence. We respect you both so much and feel it an honor that you came to our home. We do hope you will come back sometime soon when just the four of us can spend more time together."

Again, we thanked her for the invitation and stated a mutual desire to spend more time together.

"Nora, Red," said Dr. Monroe, "it is just like old times to see you. We hope you had a good time tonight and that you will come to see us in our new home down here. By the way, Red, we have a pond in front of our house and you can fish. Do come to see us soon."

We congratulated him on his new association and wished him the best of luck in the new location. Empty promises were made as to checking out his fishing site.

Next in line stood Dr. Monroe's wife, with whom Nora has spent many hours involving menial tasks such as childcare and diaper changing. She got straight to the point of the entire evening as she commented,

"Send us some business!"

Doctor Tom

Dr. Tom, an old-time dentist, came from the school of thought that to deal with a dental problem one must use an extraction forceps. A huge man, he looked strong enough to lick a lion with a licorice stick. If Dr. Tom ever got his hand into your mouth, your tooth vanished. His brand of dentistry sometimes hurt badly, but he never intended harm. His gruff demeanor belied a kindly nature.

A friend of mine, following medical advice, went to Dr. Tom to get all his teeth pulled. He got the picture of the old dentist's nature when Dr. Tom told him, "Now, son, I'm going to be just as kind to you as one man can be to another, and still pull his damned old teeth."

It often puzzled me why my friend never completed his dental appointments, until I had a chance to see Dr. Tom at work. He began to bring patients to our hospital, where I gave anesthesia, for whole-mouth extractions under anesthesia. With his size and strength, even with his best efforts not to be rough, he could not be otherwise.

It never ceased to amaze the old practitioner that the anesthetic could actually be put into a vein. More than once he asked me, "Doctor, do you mean to tell me you're putting that medicine 'di-reck-uh-ly in the suck-uh-lation'" (directly in the circulation)?

Well, that's a thumbnail sketch of Dr. Tom and now for the rest of the story:

For one year, I served as president of the local Chamber of Commerce. At the time, plans were being discussed for the location of Interstate Highway 85. There were three proposed routes, each with not-so-exciting names: the "Northern Route," the "Middle Route" and the "Southern Route." Our Chamber of Commerce stood strictly in favor of the Middle Route. Honesty compels me to say the major reason for our preference lay in the fact that it came closer to us and served our needs better. But we had a number of other good reasons and were ready, willing and able to defend our position on any front.

Someone made an appointment with Marvin Griffin, then governor of Georgia, for a group made up of representatives from all those chambers of commerce who were advocating the Middle Route. As president of the Winder Chamber of Commerce, I went to Atlanta with this group.

Gov. Griffin heard us only briefly before he told us, "Thank you for coming, but decisions of this nature are made by the highway board, and not by the Governor. Mr. John Quillian from Gainesville is the chairman of my Highway Board," he added.

We were unceremoniously sent packing to see Mr. Quillian.

Mr. Quillian, likewise, took little of our time. "Gentlemen," he informed us, "I represent the Ninth District of Georgia on this highway board and I intend to see Interstate 85 go through the Ninth District every inch it can possibly be made to go."

In other words, giving us no chance for rebuttal, he favored the Northern Route. Dejectedly, we made the return trip to Winder.

That night at our hospital medical staff meeting, a fellow member of the staff asked me, "What about our superhighway?"

"Well, fellows," came my sad reply, "it looks as if we've lost it unless we can hold off the decision until a new governor is elected. The only reason for any hope is because Georgia and South Carolina are about 12 miles apart in their proposals as to where the highway would cross the state lines. Perhaps something will work out because of that."

Dr. Tom asked indignantly, "What the hell do you want it for?"

"Dr. Tom," came my reply, "it would be nice to have to drive only 10 or 15 miles to get on a superhighway and go into Atlanta."

Holding up his hand as if he were swearing in court, Dr. Tom announced in his best Southern drawl, "I hope God never spares me to go to Atlanta again.

"You drive there in bumper-to-bumper trafic, and when you get there, you wait more than you drive. About two hours later, you finally pull up to the garage where you've been parking for 40 years, and you see a sign as big as this building that says, 'Sorry, all places filled,' "I've got to the point where I just pull up in their driveway and get out of my car and leave it running," he added defiantly.`

"The parking lot attendant will come out and yell, 'Hey, you can't do that!'

"And I say, 'Looks like I've done done it.'

"Then my wife will say," he said, (now beginning a mocking, syrupy-sweet, high voice) "'Honey, you had better not do that. You won't have no car when you come back.'

"Then I say, 'What the hell good is it? You can't drive it and you can't park it!'"

[Author's Note:] For those who are interested, we did hold off the decision on the location of I-85 until a new governor came into office. As it happened, the middle route went near a farm owned by the new head-of-state. It managed nicely to go through an edge of Barrow County and northward, with the help of a small offset in the highway, by the governor's farm to hook up with the South Carolina section at the desired location, and our problem resolved.

You can now drive 10 miles, get on a superhighway and go the 40 plus miles to Atlanta in less than an hour...but when you get there, as Dr. Tom said, you still "can't drive it and you can't park it!"

A Promise Breaker

Winder is a unique town with little class distinction. Here, most folks know one another and appear to be more or less one large family with family fights and all that goes with it.

Uncle Bud, a small-motor repair man who specialized in lawnmowers, truly seemed to be one of the kindest and most accommodating people who ever existed. I never saw the slightest streak of malice in him, nor do I remember ever having heard him say an unkind word about any person.

Morgan Mooney, better known to me as Papa, worked as a bus driver for the Trailways Bus System where he logged more than two-and-a-half million miles without a chargeable accident. Papa and I were as close as brothers and were together every time an opportunity existed. We had a special agreement when we were together: all the driving would be done by me, and the medical practice would be his job.

My operating-room conversation became so filled with stories about Papa and me, that a nurse-anesthetist from Atlanta once questioned,"Is there such a person as Papa, or is he just a figment of your imagination like Marcel Ledbetter is to Jerry Clower?"

Little did she know.

One day Papa and I were driving through Winder when we saw Uncle Bud stopped at a street corner. Papa rolled down his window and yelled, "Hey, Uncle Bud. Doc and me want to make an agreement with you. If you don't drive no buses or do no medical practice, we won't work on no lawnmower." Uncle Bud readily agreed.

A few days later, while Nora went to Callaway Gardens to help chaperone a group of kids from our church, I had started mowing the front lawn when the starter-generator fell off the lawnmower. As I struggled to replace the unit, the phone rang. Nora sounded frantic as she reported the church bus had broken down! They were stranded in the boondocks on this sultry summer day with a busload of restless kids. My instructions were to borrow a bus from another church, and come pick them up.

My focus had always been to do exactly what Nora asked regardless of (or perhaps for fear of) the consequences, so I quit working on my lawnmower and began to drive a bus—thereby breaking both parts of our agreement with Uncle Bud.

After the church kids had been rescued, Uncle Bud learned what had happened. He warned me in his gentle voice, "Well, I guess I'll just have to start practicing medicine."

A few weeks later, the local radio station announced that a Winder doctor's medical bag had been stolen from his automobile. This prompted a call from me to the chief of police telling him I knew a perfect suspect for this crime. Uncle Bud had just begun to practice medicine and seemed too cheap to buy a bag.

I never heard any results of his investigation into this serious crime. I wonder why?

I Had Rather Shave

A spinal anesthetic seemed appropriate for this particular pregnant patient so I would be free to assist Dr. Graves with her emergency Cesarean section. Normally, my duty would have been to give general anesthesia, but no other assistant stood available on this holiday.

We were aware she had a huge amount of amniotic fluid (the fluid that surrounds the baby in the mother's womb) which meant one of us would get very wet when the fluid escaped through the incision.

After administering the spinal anesthetic and before scrubbing to assist in the surgery, a small turn of a positioning crank caused the operating table to tilt ever so slightly away from my side. As a result, when the incision penetrated into the uterus, most of the escaping fluid and blood released on Dr. Graves side of the table.

His sterile gown and scrub suit were wet and bloody messes at the completion of the procedure. Dr. Graves looked down at the ugly sight, then looked at the nurses and said quite innocently, "I had rather shave every day."

I joined him in that affirmation.

Perfect Planning?

Charlie Saunders and I were closest friends. His wife, Eunice, became Nora's constant companion and confidante. In addition, for more than 30 years, she served as my chief office assistant. Our families' lives were intricately entangled both at work and in the church, and our children became almost like brothers and sisters. Many evenings were shared with our families united at one home or the other.

On this particular occasion, we were spending the evening at the Saunders home when Eunice and Nora reminded me of a house call I had promised to make that evening. My car lay dormant in a garage and the car dealer had provided a gas-guzzling loaner. Since the call seemed no emergency, I did not want to go. The women insisted, reminding me of my promise. Finally, I gave in. "Okay. I'll go if all of you go with me."

So eight people, four adults and four children, piled in the car for a house-call after 9:30 pm.

By the time we made one other check-in visit, my watch read after ten when we reached the home. A violent summer thunderstorm raged as I dashed to the front door. The family had gone to bed, but got up to let me in. I gave the old man his shot of B-12 to perk him up after a prolonged illness.

As I made the dash back to the car, it neared 11:00 p.m. and the children were restless. Drenching wet, I reached for the keys in the ignition where I had left them. No keys were to be found. My youngest child had pulled them out and dropped them somewhere in the car.

Our frantic search of the crowded car produced no keys but, by accident, we discovered a turn of the switch housing without a key would crank the motor. Thank God, we were on our way.

We had not backed out of the yard in that driving rain before another problem reared its head. The right rear tire was flat and the spare was in the car's trunk which could only be unlocked with the lost key. Every other person in the car sought desperately for the keys while Charlie and I stood outside in the rain to allow room for the search.

Finally, the keys were located and we opened the trunk. Charlie and I took the spare tire from the trunk and changed it in that driving rain. Occasionally, a flash of lightning even let us see what we were doing in that pitch-black dark with no flashlight. No words can describe how wet the two of us were.

We had made less than one-half mile of the return trek home when, well after midnight, the engine sputtered. That gas-guzzler had used all of the two-dollars worth of gas—about 6 gallons—I had put in it, not wanting to fill up a loaner car. We were out of gas. Nothing was open for miles around and it still rained quite hard.

I had no other choice but to set out on foot and see what could be found. About a quarter-of-a-mile down the road stood Mr. Beardle's store. I had treated some of his family, so I knew him. His residence attached to the backside of the store with his front porch on the side. For the first time in an hour or so, I was in the dry as I knocked on Mr. Beardle's front door.

Either he had gone deaf or he was not at all eager to answer my persistent knocking at that hour of the night. Just as my hope of arousing him faded, Mr. Beardle opened the door. His greeting of me did not match the cheery one I usually expected from this fine old country storekeeper and farmer. My happiness on seeing him seemed to far exceed his on seeing me.

Our dilemma was quickly explained and Mr. Beardle located two glass, gallon jugs. He unlocked his gasoline pumps and filled the two jugs with the precious amber liquid we so desperately needed. Claiming he had no change, Mr. Beardle refused any pay.

There seemed to be more spring in my step as I made the return trip to the crowded, pulsating car full of disgruntled kids and adults. Spontaneous cheers went up as the motor leapt to life again, this time actually at the urging of an ignition key.

Nora and Eunice never seemed to feel sorry for me and the soaking I took that night. Instead, they would say, "You should have been in the car with those wild, sleepy children."

For some reason, they hardly ever went on any more nighttime house-calls with me.

CHAPTER 4

SPORTS AND SPORTING STORIES

*B*EING A CHILD IN *a large and quite poor family during the depression era required me to begin regular gainful work at an early age. Neither time nor money was available for things as nonproductive as team sports or outdoor sporting endeavors like hunting and fishing. Dad hunted for the family, and would sometimes take me along, but only to help carry his kill. In school, being the youngest and most immature in my class meant my always being the last one reluctantly chosen for a team. I remember the humiliation of "You take him." "No, you take him!"*

These facts caused me to come to adulthood with boyish dreams in the entire sporting arena unfulfilled and virtually unexplored. I had a keen desire to explore them to know if I could be as good in real life as I had been in my dreams. Painful experiences as a too juvenile caddy made me certain golf was not my game; football was eliminated because of its inherent danger to the support of my family. After short experience and minimal success, tennis and softball were abandoned because of fluid accumulation on my right knee.

This left the outdoor sports of hunting and fishing as my areas of personal involvement, and the role as physician and advisor to young people fortunate enough to be in team sports as my area of expertise. It also led to many stories, a few of which I would like to share.

They're Coming To Take Me Away, Ha Ha!

I filled the position of team physician for Winder athletic teams for 19 full seasons. Although the job carried no pay even when it required treatment of injuries, I regarded it as a serious commitment. In my opinion, no athletic contest, especially a football game, should go on without my being present and we usually found a way for me to attend.

During a portion of that time, my partner and I did all of the anesthesia for the local hospital. With the surgery schedule so full on this particular day, it naturally fell my turn to be on call to give anesthesia. Winder-Barrow High School also had a football game scheduled in Commerce for that night.

The weather was pleasant on my arising that morning, and I chose a light suit to wear to the hospital. I had planned to change to heavier clothing before going into the night air for the football game. Little did I know!

Emergency after emergency forced me to spend the entire day in the operating room. The last case ended at 7:30 p.m., the exact time the football kicked off in Commerce, about a 40 minute drive from Winder. I had no time for a trip home to change clothes.

I made a hasty decision to wear the green operating room scrub suit under my regular suit for a layered clothing effect. I rolled up the legs of the scrub pants, put on my lighter-than-desired suit and literally roared off to Commerce.

The football field in Commerce appeared to me to be located on the back side of nowhere. It seemed you had to make a dozen or more turns to get there. Having never been able to negotiate this maze without driving all over town, I deemed it a good idea to ask directions and possibly save some time. I drove into a service station and jumped out of my car.

In those days, service stations really lived up to their names by giving service. The attendant saw me drive up and came outside to care for my needs. I made my request for directions to the football field and, still making every effort to save time, backed toward my automobile while he gave those directions. My eyes were fixed on the attendant as he used his hands to point out what turns should be taken.

With my back to the car, I felt for the door handle, opened the door, got into the car and reached for the steering wheel. To my great chagrin, my hands hit—not the steering wheel—but the back of the front seat. I had climbed into the back seat of the car!

Trying to cover my embarrassment, I said something very original and clever like, "My goodness, I'm in the back seat!"

Quickly, I jumped out of the car, got in the front seat, cranked the engine and, once again, tried to race off to the game. In my haste to go, my car motor died, not once, not twice, but three times before I exited the service station lot.

His directions were excellent, but it was already halftime when I arrived at the football field. As I entered the stadium, they were paging me to care for one of our players who had been injured. As I scurried across the football field in the direction of the field house, I looked down and could not believe what my sight revealed. Hanging down about three inches below the trousers of my suit, the legs of those green operating room pants were shining brightly.

Surely my face must have outshined the stadium lights as it glowed in their relative dark with that discovery.

My mind flashed back, and it made me shutter even worse to think about what must have been the thoughts of the service station attendant after my unbelievable demonstration at his place. Certainly, he must have envisioned me as a lunatic escaped from the mental hospital several miles down Highway 441 at Milledgeville, and himself lucky to see me go with no bodily harm to him.

You can rest assured this deeply embarrassed physician kept a constant watch the entire second half of the football-game for the "*man in the little white coat.*"

I Want To Play

Near the end of one of our high school football team's more successful seasons, I went to check on the team's practice immediately after my last patient cleared the office. On this day, to my surprise, practice had been cut short and the team gathered, each with a handful of cookies, around a large container of lemonade.

"What are we celebrating?" I asked.

"It's Bobby's birthday," came a chorus of answers.

Bobby, a star linebacker on the team, had one more year left in school. He had been one of the keys to our good season, and we had high hopes for another good year with his fine play.

"How old are you today, Bobby?" I asked with sincere interest.

"Nineteen," was his unwanted answer.

"No, Bobby," I teased disappointedly. "You're 18."

"No sir,' came the respectful answer from our star player. "I am 19 today."

"No, Bobby. Surely you mean 18. if you're 19 now, that means you can't play football next year!" I gulped my retort.

"Uh. Come to think of it, my grandmother has always said they put the wrong date on my birth certificate. She says I am only 18 today, but Momma and Daddy disagree," he responded uncertainly.

I thought nothing more about the conversation until news came to me that Bobby had petitioned the local court to change the birth-year on his birth certificate. His grandmother had signed an affidavit of her opinion and given some proof to back it. From idle chatter had come the possibility of a significant change in this student's life, and I bore some responsibility for it.

I buttonholed Bobby on our next meeting. "Bobby, I understand you have petitioned the court to change your birth date and make you eligible to play next year."

"Yes, sir," he replied with a grin. "She has always told me they had the wrong year."

"But, Bobby, we need to think this thing through because it will affect things for the rest of your life.'

"Yes, sir. Doc, but I want to play," Bobby responded with obvious misery.

"I know you want to play, and I want you to play also, but we do need to look at the future consequences. For instance, you will be eligible for the Army draft one more year," I reasoned.

"But, Doc, I want to play," came his only answer.

"And," I continued, "when you get old enough to retire, you will have to work an extra year before you can draw Social Security. You see, there are consequences far beyond today you must carefully consider."

"But, Doc, I want to play." He repeated his answer in assured tones, then he added, "I am perfectly willing to wait a year before I can draw Social Security and to be eligible for the Army draft for another year. Football is my life right now. I want to play!"

The case continued its way before the judge who saw merit in the grandmother's petition. Bobby's birth certificate was changed and, the next year, he and Ronnie Saunders made one of the best linebacking duos in the history of the Winder-Barrow High School.

This happened more than 40 years ago and, of course, there have been questions in my mind as to whether my idle chatter had brought harm to Bobby's life,

Now, he is nearly 60, and made this statement to me recently. "Doc, I've done some dumb things in my life, but that does not rank as one of them. That became the most fun year of my life and it kept me in school where I probably learned more than in any year before. I would not have graduated if I could not play football. If I had the same chance now, I'd do it over again."

It is peculiar and frightening how entire lives can be changed by a single chance remark.

Zip

The little boy, at that time in the second grade, had been spared what some call the mutilation of a circumcision procedure at birth. On one particular day, he had considerable regret about that omission in his past. A small tag of his foreskin got caught in the zipper of his pants as he completed a visit to the restroom.

After some quite painful and notably unsuccessful efforts to correct the situation, the principal of his elementary school, Mr. John Peterman, brought him to our office. At the office, this sad and painful situation came under the skilled and watchful care of my associate, Dr. Richard Forrest "Dick" Graves.

Dr. Graves had seen a a patient with this problem on a previous occasion and knew the simple solution for it. He took a pair of scissors, cut across the zipper below the problem area and, causing virtually no pain, the zipper almost fell apart.

Because other boys in the school were keenly aware of this painful, yet humorous, situation, our thus freed patient acquired the nickname of "Zip."

Imagine my amused grin several years later when "Zip" became an emerging seventh grade football star. As the cheerleaders began to chant in unison, "Run, Zip, run," *I could not help but smile and wonder, Do they know?*

The Preacher's Story

Papa Mooney had a few Beagle hounds trained to run rabbits. Listening to the sound of his dogs baying as they chased those elusive critters over Barrow or Jackson County's beautiful rolling hills became one of my favorite pastimes. Certainly, the poor little frightened rabbit had nothing to fear from my shotgun. The three volleys allowed me on sighting the speeding hare served only to warn him of the danger from other shotguns, and spurred him to run faster.

On one occasion, Rev. Bill Bowen, pastor of the First Methodist Church, had joined our party. He stood perhaps a hundred yards from my chosen location as we waited for the dogs to turn the quarry out of the woods and into the clearing where we waited. Suddenly, the object of our hunt popped into the clearing. I knew he was too far away for my gun to be effective, but I fired three shots anyhow. I rushed to the spot where the rabbit had run, calling the dogs to put them on the fresh scent.

About that time, Papa came to where Rev Bowen had stationed himself, and asked, "Preacher, where is Doc?"

Rev Bowen responded, "I don't know. The last time I saw him, he was chasing the rabbit and outrunning the dogs. As they went over the hill, here ran the rabbit…here goes Doc…and there come the dogs."

Technically, he was correct. But my preacher friend would never have made those remarks if he knew what type of ribbing he opened up for me to get from Papa for as long as Papa lived. Or would he?

Papa's Other Choice

On another occasion, Papa and I were rabbit hunting alone. We had planned to spend the entire day in that pursuit, so we went prepared, each with a huge sack lunch in our hunting jackets.

Hunting is much more pleasant if your boots and breeches are dry and you are not worried about freezing to death. Therefore, our custom evolved to begin a hunt about nine in the morning with the dew disappeared and the weather warmer.

On this particular occasion, we had just arrived at our hunting site and released the dogs. With the crisp morning air and the totally clear sky, it seemed a perfect day for that pastime. After we loaded our guns, we crossed the roadside ditch and entered our friend's field for our day of pleasure.

When hunting together, hunters usually separate 50 or more yards from one another to give better coverage of the area being canvassed and to lessen the danger of shooting one another. Papa and I were in this separation process and just crossing the first terrace in the field when he pulled out his lunch and took a big bite of a sandwich.

"Papa, why are you eating already?" I inquired. "We will be here all day. Shouldn't you wait?"

Papa's reply came immediately and sounded logical. "Well, Doc, it's like this," he grinned. "I'd rather have it on my stomach than to have it on my mind."

Fishing With Doc

We built a small cabin on Lake Lanier near Gainesville, Georgia, shortly after the lake filled. I wanted to spend as much time as I could on the lake fishing or playing in the water with my children. My fishing buddies were numerous and the company of each one brought me pleasure. But with this one character who frequently became my fishing partner, it seemed something happened on each occasion we fished together. Royce McNeal served as Minister of Music and Youth at the First Baptist Church of Winder.

One time, we left the car in a public parking area. After an evening of fishing, we came back to our car about midnight and found someone had stolen the tires—wheels and all—from the front of my car. Even though they left the front of the car sitting on the ground, it escaped my notice until the steering wheel would not turn when I started to drive away.

Fortunately, James Lay had joined us late and had driven his van. We used this van to drive into Gainesville where a helpful policeman aroused a reluctant tire dealer from his sleep at about 2 a.m. so we could buy two tires and wheels.

It has always been a mystery to me why that dealer did not wish to honor a sale price on those tires and wheels. We had given him such an early start on his next wonderful day.

A REGULAR STICK-IN-THE-MIND

Another time, Royce, James Lay and I got stuck—hopelessly stuck we thought—in the red mud in front of my cabin. We walked about a half-mile to the house of a neighbor called Jody. His actions and speech mirrored a true North Georgia hills person with a speech impediment. We asked Jody to take us to Winder and told him we would send a wrecker to get the car next morning.

Jody had other ideas. He intended to take his pickup truck and pull my car out.

Not wanting to have both vehicles stuck in the mud so we had no possibility to get home, we objected. "But, Jody, what if your truck gets stuck?"

Jody replied simply, "If hit won't come out, we will jes' buhn (burn) hit."

'Do you have a chain," I questioned?

"Hi got mo' chain than de chain man got," responded Jody proudly. He gathered several lengths of chain from his front yard and got into his pickup truck.

It continued to rain lightly as I climbed into the bed of the pickup truck. Jody and my two companions climbed into the front seat, then Jody beckoned to me. He used an oxymoron I had never heard before as he said, "Come on up here and set wid us. Dis here is a big old widdle (little) pickup truck."

When we reached my hopelessly entrenched automobile, Jody instructed me to get into the car and start the motor, as he hitched his truck to my car using a long chain. Royce climbed on its back bumper to give my car more traction.

When Jody put his truck in gear and raced the motor, its wheels spun furiously and the sticky red mud flew just as furiously, covering everything in its path. Royce realized his danger and ducked his head to keep the mud out of his eyes. His entire scalp with its sparse hair turned red, not only from mud, but from the speed with which that mud hit his near bald pate.

On about the third try, the car came out onto solid ground.

Jody's report of how things went was simple. "Hi jest give hit a widdle jek. Den hi jest give hit anudder widdle jek and felt hit move. Den hi jest give hit hell!"

Jody got us out of that tight spot, but it meant another time of getting home in the early hours of morning from a routine fishing trip with Royce.

American Ingenuity

As Royce and I backed into our parking place near my cabin to start our fishing for the day, I felt a slight bump underneath when the car touched a grass-covered stump. The car easily drove off the stump and we thought nothing of the incident. We fished until dark-thirty, as usual. When we started home that night, the car cranked easily, went about 50 feet and simply died. We nearly died also, because neither of us knew a thing about mechanics and pitch-black darkness had set in by that time.

Trying to make the most of a bad situation, we found a leftover 100 foot roll of electrical wire from the wiring of my cabin. We secured a table lamp from the cabin and straight-wired each limb of its plug to one end of the electrical wire. Each bared individual wire of the other end then we inserted into each side of an electrical outlet on the cabin porch. Thus blessed with light, I crawled under the car.

After much search, I located a copper tubing line with a short piece of rubber tubing attached, obviously disconnected from something. As I blew hard into the rubber hose and released it, lo and behold, gasoline started to pour in a large stream onto the ground. The hose was clamped off temporarily by bending the rubber part with my fingers.

"Royce," I instructed, "get my medical bag from the car."

He got my bag.

"Open it and get my emergency suture kit," were my next instructions, "It's the one wrapped in a white towel and laying on top."

Royce found the kit

"Now, open that," I requested.

Royce complied.

"Now, hand me a hemostat, one of those medical clamps, to stop this 'hemorrhage of gasoline," I said.

The clamp was supplied and applied, then, the search began for the other end of the fuel line. Finally, I located it just below the motor where it had disappeared through a hole in the frame of the car. I fished it out.

Holding both ends of the fuel-line, I still could not join the two ends together using the attached piece of rubber tubing. It appeared to be too short.

"Royce," came my instructions again, "get my stethoscope out of the bag and the scissors from my emergency kit."

He got them.

"Now, cut an eight-inch piece of tubing from the stethoscope."

The fuel line was spliced with this tubing and it got us home.

The major ensuing problem became my chronic backache that developed, not from the work as a mechanic, but by having to bend over so far to listen to patients while using a short stethoscope.

Incidentally, while the fiasco with the severed fuel supply line was occurring, we could hear a boat that sounded as if it were going around in circles on the lake. The voices of two drunk men could clearly be heard in conversation,

"Do you see that light up there?" asked one of them, having obviously seen my rigged lamp.

'Yeah, I see the light," came the reply.

"That's where Dr. Skelton lives," continued the first voice. "He's a good old son of a bitch."

Now, I ask you, should I be happy because he called me good or should I complain about what he called me otherwise?

A Fisherman's Oxymoron

Santiago is a bivocational Baptist preacher who resides in Temuco, Chile. We had become acquainted when, while on mission trips in his country, I held a series of revival meetings in his church. On the occasion of this story, Penny (the present Mrs. Skelton) and I were vacationing in his country and had received an invitation to dinner at the home of my long-term friend.

Santiago speaks no English, and my minuscule knowledge of Spanish dictated the need for an interpreter. The delicious dinner with its light conversation had been consumed and the after-dinner conversation on more important subjects had begun. Naturally, the subject soon turned to fishing.

I had completed my tale about Papa Mooney and me when, as novices, we located such a cache of Florida seatrout that, by the third day, the professional guides were following us to our fishing hole.

When it came Santiago's turn to speak, his tale revolved around fishing with some friends, and depending on their catch for dinner. Late in the day, they had caught no fish. They met a man with many fish who told them he used larvae from a wasp nest as bait. Each of Santiago's party got his own wasp nest and there were plenty of fish caught for their meal.

Both of our fishing stories were rendered completely secondary by the first four words of our interpreter as he told Santiago's tale:

"This lie is true!"

CHAPTER 5

SIMPLY PICTURESQUE SPEECH

IN MY MORE THAN 40 years of practice there have been many truly classic descriptions made by patients concerning their illness and its symptoms. The very first statement made by patients and their initial complaint are the source of classic quotes, so careful attention is always given these two items. Because there have been notable exceptions to this rule, I have also learned to hear exactly what a patient says and then attempt to interpret what is meant by their statements.

Believe me, these two are by no means always the same!

By listening in this manner, I have gathered a number of stories that are certainly worth repeating. Several of the word forms and idioms are from a rapidly disappearing era and culture.

Whereas it may not be all bad that the era and culture are disappearing, it would sadden me to know the humorous and picturesque speech patterns of the time would all have to vanish with them. This is my effort to salvage a few of these word forms and idioms:

All Inclusive Pain

A feverish young lady with the flu giving her presenting symptoms: "My hair hurts. My toenails hurt. And everything in between hurts."

Total Agony

Another young lady with a case of influenza giving her initial complaint: "If it don't hurt, I ain't got it."

How About Your Shadow?

A middle-aged man with degenerative arthritis who eventually had to have a total hip replacement: "I just can't walk. I would stumble over a tooth pick!"

These Cheap Time Pieces

A young lady with a several-day history of nausea, cramps and diarrhea: "I've got a 24-hour virus with a stopped clock."

The "Locked" Bowels

A young man who also had a several day history of cramps and diarrhea: "My bowels are locked—in the open position."

Drunk Again

A 70 year old man with dizziness and weakness: "I can't get my legs and my head sober."

That's a Digestive System

An 84 year old man bragging about the state of his wife's health, and especially about her good digestion: "I believe she could eat fried horseshoes."

A Good Toothache?

An elderly man with high blood pressure and severe arthritis trying to describe the intense pain he had in his hip joint: "Compared to that pain, a toothache would feel good."

Watch Those Grasshoppers

A 93 year old man drove 75 miles with his wife and stayed overnight in a local motel to see me. Somehow he thought that I could and would convince the Geogia State Patrol to give him back his driver's license. They had taken his valued permit because of multiple traffic offenses and accidents

He did not help his chance of gaining help from me in reclaiming his lost license when he gave the following complaint: "I am very unstable, any and every direction. A grasshopper could kick me over, I doubt I could pull a setting hen off her nest backward.'

Papa Seems To Be Better

Papa, the aforementioned Morgan Mooney, had a really bad case of diarrhea with nausea and vomiting for which he had been given treatment. A couple of days later, he returned and I queried, "How are you feeling now, Papa?"

"Well, Doc, I reckon I'm better," came his reply, "At least now, when I go to the bathroom, I know which end to put on the commode. Before, I had to make a choice."

Miss Lannie

Miss Lannie, an old maid, had lived into her 80's. She may well have had the most sour disposition of any patient I have ever dealt with in my office. Nevertheless, I teased and cajoled her with the same vigor as with any other patient.

When asked about her problem as she came into the office on this particular visit, she answered, "I have a very bad cold."

One of my best loved word games assumes that if something is bad in one case, the same thing may be good in another case. Therefore my next question came, "Miss Lannie, did you ever have a good cold?"

Of course, nothing funny was ever expected from this old maid who, without a moment of hesitation and in that sweet voice with which many thought she attempted to hide her sour disposition, answered, "Well, yes. When I was a young girl there was a boy who wanted to date me and I didn't want to go out with him. So, every time he would come, I would have a cold—and that was good."

I have asked the same question a thousand times before and a thousand times since. The only answer that ever approached being equally funny came from a lady who responded with, "Yes. One that I was already rid of."

However, I keep on asking. One never knows when he may unearth another pearl.

Beaten At My Own Game

Oftentimes, my patients respond to my question, "How are you today?" with, "I am better."

Even though I know the grammar is incorrect, my frequently used counter-question is, "Who are you better than?"

There have been many and varied answers to that question. It is my ardent belief you can tell something of the psychological makeup of a person by their first answer to the counter-question.

Some will squirm and timidly say, "Nobody! I'm not better than anybody else."

Some will respond, "Anybody who is in the cemetery."

Others will have no answer and appear frustrated by the fact you even asked.

Many will give the obvious answer, "I feel better than I felt when you saw me last time."

One of the problems with playing the same word game many times with many patients over many years is the fact you cannot remember all of the patients with whom you have played this certain game. This was apparently the case with Mose and me.

Mose, an intelligent, humorous, elderly man who had mild diabetes, continued his recovery from a heart attack…his second. He had improved considerably and apparently had been thinking about how he could answer in a forthright and truthful manner the question he knew I would ask.

I really think he waited for me with a baited trap when he answered my query as to how he felt with, "I'm better."

"Who are you better than?" I fell into his trap.

Mose gave a quick, studied, almost perfect reply as he said, "Most everybody…that ain't as good as I am."

With that turning of the tables, the one who began to study was me. I thought about his words and realized they could be paraphrased to say, "If they are not as good as I am, then I am better than they are." It becomes a simple statement of fact.

Who can argue with that?

Ophelia and Samantha

I loved their names almost as much as these two old ladies themselves were loved by me. Those names just seemed to flow off the tongue with a sound of rhythmic melody. Ophelia and Samantha, (they called the latter, "Manthy") were widowed sisters who appeared to be true mountain ladies transplanted into this foothills county. Both of them were getting old but they took pride in the fact they required little help from other family members, in spite of their advanced years. Their dependence rested on God and on one another.

Eventually, time took its toll and Samantha, now into her nineties, developed Alzheimer's disease. As the saying goes, she "went completely out to lunch" mentally and had to be placed in a nursing home many miles from Winder. One day, Ophelia came into the office for a checkup and, as I always did, I asked about the condition of Samantha. Ophelia's reply went very much like this:

"Oh, Manthy, she's just plumb pitiful. I go up thar to see her an' she don't even know me. I go out of th' room, an' when I come back, she don't even 'member I've been thar.

"But come to think about it, Manthy may be better off'n I am, 'cause here I've got all these worriments and besetments, and Manthy don't seem to have none."

As Ophelia taught me, "Come to think about it," there may be some benefits (from Alzheimer's disease) after all…to the patient.

An Unlikely Cure

Mrs. Pipers' speech reflected her lack of education. A short, stocky, somewhat obese woman, her jaw hung down with a jowl-like effect that gave her an appearance akin to a bulldog. Perhaps, this relaxed lower jaw was the anatomical reason for her speech being quite explosive. If you were in front of Mrs. Pipers when she spoke, you had better duck or you might be spattered with snuff-juice that emitted from her mouth with each utterance.

Mrs. Pipers loved me like one of her own children and refused to see any other doctor regardless of how sick she might be. Many times I scolded her for not getting prompt medical attention only to hear her patented excuse, "But Doc, you wuzn't here."

One day, Mrs. Pipers came into the office and, when asked about her problem, she replied in her most explosive fashion. "Lord, Doc, I'm a heap better now than I wuz yestiddy! Yestiddy, I thought I wuz a'gonna die. It wuz m' belly, Doc. I thought m' belly wuz a'gonna kill me!

"Doc, I done everythang I knowed to do. I taken some asmin (aspirin) tablets; I taken some Alky Sulkas (Alka Seltzer). Doc, I even taken a wash-out (an nema) and th' thang whut finally give me some ease wuz some of them color-yore-water pills!"

Now, this writer would like to see you keep a straight face all through a soliloquy such as that when you're face-to-face in a small examining room. I don't claim to have even tried.

The Tense Test

The young man had not been seen before in my office practice. As he told me his story of abdominal pain and heartburn associated with some nausea and rare vomiting, I reasoned that he might well have an ulcer. Knowing there is often a nervous component to ulcer disease, I questioned him, "Tell me, friend. Are you tense?"

His quick answer to my query caught me totally unprepared, "Well, Doctor, I don't know whether you would call it tense or not, but right now, if I had a 20-penny-nail in my rectum, you could not pull it out with a John Deere tractor."

That story has been passed around several panels of experts and there is a large preponderance of opinion that he most likely met the definition of "tense."

Faye Hicks, the Barrow County mental health nurse, has helped me design a very specific test for tenseness on the basis of this story. We have most of the needed equipment. We have a 20-penny-nail and a rope, but to this date we have been unable to borrow a tractor from the county to carry out the test.

Perhaps you can help us with this need.

CHAPTER 6

FUNCTIONAL MISPRONUNCIATIONS

*M*OST PATIENTS FEEL WE *doctors deal in confusing terminology too often. The words we use are often extremely difficult for lay people to pronounce—much less to spell or to have much idea as to their meaning. Yet, thoughtlessly, we sometimes pass out technical terms indiscriminately and their meaning is often misunderstood by the lay public.*

Well, here is good news for you. The meanings, pronunciations and spelling are not always easy for us, either. My remembrance is vivid of the young female medical student who, when we were studying about Hytadidiform (pronounced as hi-ta-did-I-form) moles, continued to call them "Hi-daddy-diddy-form moles" even after she had become a senior medical student.

So you see, the language is not easy for us, either. There will be no effort here to tell you about some of my own blunders as we learned a totally new set of terms...almost a new language.

Dirty Laundry Don't Take No Doctor's Orders

As would be expected, among lay persons, mispronunciations of medical terms is the rule rather than the exception. This is especially true in a rural setting. Therefore, I am never surprised by and rarely remember the many and varied mispronunciations of medical and other terms made by my patients.

For example, I have heard the prostate gland referred to as:

> *the "prospect gland,"*
>
> *the "prosperous gland,"*
>
> *"my phosphates,"*
>
> *the "prostrate,"*
>
> *the "project gland,"*

And an almost endless list of incorrect pronunciations.

There is, however, that rare occurrence of what I choose to call a "functional mispronunciation." My definition of this term, which I have never seen in the literature, is as follows: "that perfectly delightful situation where, in my opinion, the mispronounced term is more fitting, proper and descriptive than the usual medical terminology."

There are some frequently quoted sound-alike terms like the familiar "hip-to-rectum-operation" instead of hysterectomy, but none of these mispronunciations with which I am familiar seems actually more descriptive than the medical term.

With the exception of the seemingly English-speaking-worldwide use of "Oldtimer's disease" for "Alzheimer's disease," functional mispronunciations are exceedingly rare, I have collected only an extremely limited number of them in all my years of practice. My entire small collection of these treasured findings is now proudly submitted in the pages that follow:

Proper Name For An Electrocardiogram

The old lady was not usually my patient, so when her family called me to her home to examine and treat her because of chest pain, I felt an obligation to obtain an adequate history of all her past medical problems and treatment. She made every effort to provide me with all the needed information.

In response to my question as to what diagnostic procedure had been performed, she replied, "Oh, Dr. Randolph has already taken seven different heart-a-grams on me."

If you ask me, the name should be changed immediately, and my vote is for her version. After all, an electrocardiogram is simply a tracing or graph of the electrical activity of the heart and her term is more descriptive.

Electrocardiogram is just too technical.

Did You Say "Strep" Throat?

Limousene…honest to God, her real name. The grapevine has it she entered this world as the sixteenth child in a family where her parents had made a decision to give all their children names beginning with the letter "L." You can easily see how it would be entirely possible for her to come by the name of Limousene.

At least, it beats the other local story about the eleventh child in a Barrow Country family given the name of "Leben," but that's another story entirely.

Limousene reported to the office one day with a high fever and sore throat. She looked ill. "Limousene, what in the world is the matter with you?" I asked.

Her answer surprised me. "Dr. Skeleton, I think my throat's done stripped."

Was I evermore impressed! Her term so much better describes the havoc raised by the Streptococcus infection of the tonsils than our unimaginative term of "strep throat." Anyone who has ever suffered from this awful ailment knows Limousene hit the descriptive nail directly on the head, and my vote is for her term to be adopted.

Hiatal Hernia?

One of the more commonly mispronounced medical terms is "hiatal hernia." This is a hernia through the diaphragm, the breathing muscle at the base of the rib cage that separates the chest from the abdomen. This hernia usually occurs just underneath the breast bone near its lower tip when a part of the stomach actually slides up through a hole, or "hiatus," in the diaphragm, and into the chest. Over one-half of the people above 40 have this type hernia, so you can see it is quite a common malady.

Because it's so common, many lay people hear the term and try to pronounce the words. So you get many mispronunciations. The following come off the top of my mind:

"Hyena hernia."

"Hightail hernia."

"Hiccup hernia."

"High hernia."

But, the one that sticks in my mind, and I believe doctors should install as the official name of this problem, is one given to me by a patient. He claimed to have a 'high-up hernia."

That accurately describes the problem, and the higher up it gets, the more problems you have with it. Let's get on with the name change.

Say No To Vertigo

The lady had been ill for some time and had been seen by several doctors including my partner, Dr. Graves. Her worst problem seemed to be dizziness—a problem for which we doctors use the non-descriptive term "vertigo." In taking her history to determine the direction my treatment should proceed, I asked her routinely, "For what problem has Dr. Graves been treating you?"

With no thought of humor, her immediate reply blurted, "Oh, he was treating me for the 'whirlygo of the head.'"

If one has ever suffered from this problem, he is forced to admit, "She got it right." Your head absolutely goes in a whirl. It also often produces a ringing sensation in the ears sometimes associated with mild to severe nausea.

After all these years, this certainly is the greatest improvement in descriptive diagnostic medical terms I have ever heard, and my vote is for its immediate adoption in the medical lexicon.

CHAPTER 7

Just funny stories

Triply innocent

As a resident physician working in the emergency room in a hospital in Louisiana, I saw a patient who had multiple lacerations over a large portion of his body. Apparently, his assailant employed a type of knife like those used to open cardboard boxes, and had it set so it would not cut very deep. All of his 27 incisions were fairly superficial, although some were quite long.

It did not really matter to me nor was it any of my business who made the attack on my patient, but my curiosity was aroused. Just making routine conversation, my question to him followed, "Who cut you so many times?"

"I don't rightfully know," he answered.

Greatly surprised by his answer, I responded, "Oh, come off of that stuff. Are you really trying to tell me a man cuts you 27 times and you don't even know who he is? Do I appear to you to be actually that stupid?"

He quickly retorted, "Boss Man, I didn't even see the man who cut me."

Not believing one word of his story, I continued my questioning, "How can you expect me to believe such a tale? A man cuts you this many times and you don't even see him?"

He raised his hand as if he were swearing on a Bible in a courtroom and said, "Boss Man, I'll tell you the God's truth. I was at home, settin' in my bathtub, reading my Bible, an' somebody stuck his hand in my window an' cut me!"

No more questions were asked—nor were any needed. His story was recognized immediately as the best story I would ever hear in trying to explain an injury. I paused for a time of contemplation and the moment was savored completely.

As the procedure of suturing his 27 lacerations dragged on, my mind delved deeply into his testimony. The deeper my mind dug, the more I became convinced of this man's innocence. Consider the facts:

No. 1. It occurred at home. That's innocence.

No. 2 In his bathtub. That's innocence.

No. 3 while reading his Bible. The final straw of his innocence.

That makes him triply innocent.

Of course, I still did not believe his story—not even one single word of it—but it certainly intrigued me.

Then, a thing happened that made me question a bit if I had judged my patient unfairly. About a week later, I read in one of those little printed-only-for-the-advertising scandal sheets that try to serve as medical journals, a story about a man who had come into an emergency room in a California hospital.

This man appeared bruised and beat up considerably and had been cut several times. When asked what had happened, he reported that while he took a bath, a typewriter came flying through the window and hit him. That, along with flying glass from the broken window, had caused all of his cuts and bruises.

Naturally, that story met with total disbelief.

A short time later, however, the police brought in a prisoner who had minor injuries inflicted on him as he was arrested. When hospital personnel asked for a report on their new patient's problem, the policeman explained it this way.

"We had a report saying John here," pointing to their prisoner, "had stolen a typewriter and we were chasing him down an alley. When we caught him, he claimed to be innocent, but he put up a fight before we got him subdued. When we finally got him quiet, he had no typewriter with him. We searched and searched through the whole alley and no typewriter could be found anywhere."

But you and I, dear reader, know its location, don't we?

Slide Carefully

A middle-aged black man came into the emergency room of the Louisiana hospital where I served my residency. He had a small cut on his hand that would require several stitches. His wife accompanied him, and it appeared perfectly obvious from the start who "wore the pants" in this family.

Just making conversation, I asked him, "How did you cut your hand?"

His reply came quickly—as if it had been practiced, "I was playing baseball with the brothers and I slid into the second base. We were playing in a pasture and there was all kinds of stuff laying around. You know what kind of stuff lays around in a pasture.

"Well, when I slid into second base, I slid into a knife and it cut me."

He certainly did not look like a baseball player to me. He appeared to be too old for that, and his story absolutely did not ring true.

Not that it mattered one whit nor should it really have been made any of my business, my questioning continued, "And who held the knife that cut you when you slid into second base?"

"Nobody," he replied, "Naw sir, nobody!"

His wife agreed emphatically, "Das right. Das right."

"Who do you think you are kidding?" I asked in disbelief as we sent his wife packing from the room. Hospital policy required that, for fear of contamination or of a fainting episode by the observer, no family member could remain in the emergency room while suturing or other treatment was in progress.

She had hardly left the room when my patient spoke in slightly above whispered tones, 'Boss Man, you knowed from the start I was lying to you, didn't you? My old lady done this to me. She's always cuttin' me like this.'

At that time the reason become clear to me why the wife "wore the pants" in this family.

Enough is Enough

By the time he became my patient, Jonas was living with his third wife. The first two had died, of causes unknown to me, after producing several children each. The third followed in the tradition of the first two by having a baby every year. Jonas took pride in the fact he had 21 children, and the welfare system of Georgia supported them, and him, quite well. Jonas had them convinced of his disability. He had equally well convinced me of his nighttime capability.

Being disabled, Jonas was required by the welfare system to visit a doctor every so often, and he was punctual with these visits. He always presented with the same complaints…his stomach and his back. I never found any physical findings of consequence on him, nor did any medicines ever seem to do his symptoms the slightest good.

We developed a ritual for every visit Jonas made to my office so the full effect of his complaining could be visualized. We knew exactly what those complaints would be, and made certain there was never a chair available for Jonas to sit.

Perhaps I can draw you a word picture of Jonas, who was about six feet two inches tall, droop-shouldered and rather thin, except for a protuberant abdomen. He had a long Romanesque type nose, beady eyes, pursed lips and thin, receding hair.

As he stood there to give his complaints, he would put a hand on each offending part of his anatomy and hold the hand at the spot until I began to examine him. Having only two hands, he was naturally limited to demonstrating only two complaints in this manner.

As stated before, his major complaints were always "my stomach," (grabbing his protuberant abdomen), and "my back," (placing the other on his low back). picture him in profile as he stood with one hand in front and one on his back as he added his nearly constant third complaint, "And something to make my wife's period come around."

To me, it was a hilariously comic scene.

Folks at the Public Health Department tried to do something about the excessive fertility of Jonas' wife. They prescribed birth control pills for her, having somehow missed the fact she had already become pregnant. Her pharmacist told me she took the pills faithfully throughout the entire pregnancy, in spite of his repeated warnings. I suppose she wanted not to have twins.

I am happy to report no obvious harm came from this medicine. After all these years, that child seems just as healthy as the other 20 of Jonas' offspring.

One time when Jonas complained of severe weakness, I ordered my office nurse to give him a series of injections with Vitamin B-12 and multi-B-complex over a period of several weeks. Surprisingly, he claimed to have felt much better, and elation overwhelmed me. After all, this was Jonas who had never given even the slightest indication he had been helped at all by any of many previous treatments.

My elation became short-lived when our host called me to the telephone at a bridge party one evening a few days later. Jonas' wife sounded excited as she said "Doc, you'd better come quick. My man is complaining of severe pain in his back and is plumb hysterical with short breath."

I asked her, "What has happened to Jonas? He has been doing so much better."

Her reply was, "He said he felt a heap better this mornin' an' this afternoon, he was feelin' so good that he done some work. I tole him not to do it, but he wouldn't pay me no attention at all. He just grabbed that old hoe an' he went to work in the garden an' you see what happened.

"Shoot, you won't catch me doing nothing like that. I ain't done a lick of work in more'n seven years."

The evidence of her success in persuading Jonas to refrain from physical activity, except with her, stood as overwhelming. And I don't recall any more children being brought forth from that union.

I suppose it is the same with both child bearing and with work. Enough is enough.

Getting Ready For Christmas

Lovic probably holds the record as the hardest working man the City of Winder ever hired. He became a walking map of every water, gas and sewer line for the city. That proved to be a good thing because, in those days, Winder did not have complete records of these systems. When a question arose as to the location of a utility line, the crew always sent for Lovic who would put them within two or three feet of it almost every time. Lovic appeared willing to tackle any job or respond to an emergency at any time, day or night.

Lovic's major weakness had always been his love of whiskey… any kind of whiskey from moonshine to what he called "good government liquor." He almost always had a snout nearly full, but it never seemed to affect his readiness or his ability to work. He was truly one alcoholic who seemed never to hurt anyone but himself.

One year, just before Christmas, a traffic light stopped me as I drove through downtown Winder. When I looked to my right, there strode Lovic walking down the sidewalk in his typical shuffling gait. Quickly rolling down my car window, I called to him, "Hey, Lovic, have you bought your Christmas liquor yet?"

Lovic never broke stride and, without even one-second of hesitation, he replied, "Doc, I've done bought it three times, and I'm on my way to get it again right now."

Our area was dry at the time, but just leave it to a water and sewage man to find a watering hole.

How Was He To Know?

Jerly had proved himself a hard worker who was strong as a bull. His frequent brushes with the law usually came from "dipping in the sauce," a phrase sometimes used to describe excessive alcohol intake. One beautiful spring day, Sheriff's deputies brought him into our hospital emergency room with a large laceration of his scalp that required 14 sutures. His condition at that time could be described as being about four-thirds drunk.

Under the influence of alcohol, Jerly's nature usually became quite sweet, and I found it hard to imagine anyone wanting to hurt him. "Jerly, what has happened to you?" I questioned in surprise.

He replied, "Doc, you know how it's been raining lately. Well, I plowed my garden three weeks ago, but the rain kept me from planting it and had done packed it down hard again. When I got off from work early today," I assumed he got off because he was three-thirds drunk at that time, "I decided I would plow my garden again to loosen up the soil.

"I come home an' cranked up my old John Deere tractor an' got myself all ready to plow. Well, my neighbor's garden is right there next to mine, so I decided I'd help him by plowing his garden, too.

"I had just barely got started an' was making the second round when my neighbor come up. I didn't see him, because he come up from behind me. Man, he broke off a bran' new mop handle over my head. He knocked me plumb off that tractor an' cut me like this!

"How was I s'posed to know he had *planted* his garden this morning?"

When Jerly told me this story, a mental picture came of his neighbor, a patient of mine who retired from work because of his age and poor health.

I could picture him sitting on his porch, totally exhausted and resting from his labor of planting. And then to see some drunk, regardless of how good his intentions, plowing up his work. I could absolutely understand his being upset.

Jerly told me later, "Doc, they put me in jail an' charged me with destruction of private property. After I got out of jail, the court ordered me to go back an' take my tractor out of his garden. By the time I got around to follow the court order, a couple of weeks had passed and my neighbor's garden was really growing nice an' green.

"I was still kinda' mad," continued Jerly, "so I locked down one of the rear wheels on my old tractor and made it go 'round and 'round in a circle. Man, I caused a heap of damage to his garden this time, but now, I had orders from the judge to remove my tractor and he couldn't do anything about it."

They say the road to hell is paved with good intentions. Probably Jerly just laid one of the cobblestones.

Holler "Snake"

Almost everyone called him "Snake," not Lonel, his real name. It must have been because of his thin face and somewhat beady brown eyes. He had worked on the construction crew building the Winder-Barrow Hospital and then worked in the hospital for many years as an orderly. Having helped to build it and now helping to operate it, Snake felt himself to be an integral part of the hospital. So did we.

Snake appeared jovial most of the time, and that served him well. Of course, with a nickname like Snake, Lonel often served as the butt of some sort of joke, and it seemed almost everyone in the hospital at times became a practical joker.

The funniest thing that ever happened with Snake occurred, not as a planned practical joke but an entirely, accidental happening. The stage and the timing could not have been more perfectly planned by Laurel and Hardy nor Abbott and Costello. It seems the truly funniest things are rarely planned.

Snake had entered a patient's room to give an enema. His purpose was to give a "four H" enema, which meant the enema should be "high, hot, a heck of a lot, and the patient should hold it."

The Director of Nurses knew both Snake's whereabouts and his assigned mission, but she needed to speak to him. She felt her message for Snake could not wait until his task was complete, so she went to the patient's room to have the conversation. We had an intercom system but, for some reason, she chose not to use it.

The doors to our patients rooms were heavy enough to be virtually soundproof, so our intrepid Director backed up against the door just enough to open a tiny port for sound to pass through, but not enough for her or anyone else to see inside the room. This accomplished, she called out, "Snake!"

Meanwhile, at that precise moment, Snake had inserted the enema tube into the patient's backside and begun the flow to get his business done. But with the sound of a woman's voice calling "Snake," seemingly in the room, our patient gave a startled jump and pulled out the enema tube. The contents of the enema bucket, as well as those emitted from the patient were strewn all over the patient, the bed, and assorted parts of the room.

Had it not been for the perfect timing of the Director of Nurses' entry and for Lonel's unusual nickname, the incident would have been funny only for an instant. With the way all of the pieces fit together and the perfect timing, it remains, in my opinion, one of the funniest things to ever happen in our hospital.

What is the saying about an old man having to stick something up his rear end and holler, "Snake?"

Jack's Uncle Bill

Both men had been my long-term patients. Though they shared the same last name, they were not the least bit kin as far as anyone knew. Jack exemplified the scrupulously clean, hardworking, non-imbibing family man who dreamed big dreams for his family and strove mightily to make those dreams come true.

Bill also had a family, but appeared indolent, uneducated, prone to indulge too frequently in beverage alcohol and of exceedingly poor hygiene. All he seemed to desire for his family was just enough for them to barely get by. We kidded Jack and referred to Bill as his uncle.

Jack's brother had spent several days in the hospital recovering from a heart attack. At the same time, Bill received hospital treatment for a bleeding peptic ulcer. After several days, Bill became quite confused, probably from DTs caused by alcohol withdrawal. He pulled out his IV needle, bolted from his hospital room, ran down the steps and made his exit through the emergency room door. His only attire consisted of a thin hospital gown that tied in back—the type reputed to have been designed by a doctor named Seymore Butts. It did not seem a particularly cold day, but it was certainly too chilly to be outside in such scanty attire.

About the same time as Bill made his spectacular exit, Jack came through the emergency room door to check on his brother. The nearly hysterical emergency room nurse had tried to prevent Bill's departure, but had been brushed aside.

"Please try to stop him while I call the police," she called to Jack. Being such a good citizen, Jack agreed to try.

By the time Jack got outside, Bill had about a hundred yard head start and entered a wooded area adjacent to the hospital. As it happened, Jack's house stood barely beyond those woods only one block from the hospital. Jack chose to take his car, since Bill had put that much distance between them. When he neared Bill's location, Jack pulled off the edge of the road, got out of his car and yelled to Bill, "They want you back at the hospital."

Bill refused Jack's voiced requests to come back to the hospital. Instead, he cursed loudly and began to throw rocks at Jack and his automobile.

Jack thought a lot of his car and did not want it pummeled with rocks, so he decided to get back in the car and withdraw to a safe distance where he could keep Bill in sight. The police arrived in a few minutes to relieve Jack of his sentry duty and allow him to check on his brother.

That is the real story on Jack and his Uncle Bill. Now, let me tell you the story as told by his family and so-called friends. Surely, you don't believe a person as kind as myself would ever participate in spreading anything but the pure Gospel truth about his friend. Do you?

"Daddy had been going to the hospital two or three times a day to check on Uncle Bill. I'm sure when Uncle Bill ran out of the hospital, he was thinking, "These folks are being mean to me here, and keeping me from my liquor. If I can just get through these woods to my nephew, Jack's house, he will take care of me.'

"By the time Uncle Bill saw Daddy, he had become so confused he did not recognize his own nephew. Daddy got out of the car and begged, 'Uncle Bill, Uncle Bill, please come back. You are going to catch your death of pneumonia if you stay out here dressed like that. Uncle Bill, please come back.'

"When Uncle Bill started throwing rocks, Daddy was torn between his love for Uncle Bill and his love for his car. Then he thought, 'Shucks, I'm on the same side of this argument as the car is. He could hit me as well as my car with one of those rocks. I'd better think about me and get out of here.'

"That's when he got back in the car and let the police take over.

"Daddy, you just wait and don't worry. Uncle Bill will knock on that door any day, now. He can't stay mad at his favorite nephew for very long."

For a period of time, Jack tried to set the record straight. Then he decided he could not win. When Uncle Bill was mentioned, Jack would just grin sheepishly.

Welcome, Hot Flashes

On one of those bone chilling nights so unusual for the beautiful State of Georgia in November, the numbers on the football scoreboard revealed our Winder team was being soundly beaten again. That only made the cold more unbearable.

Nora and Sue were huddled together under a blanket, not nearly thick enough for the unseasonably cold weather. Sue, our neighbor from across the street, suffered from change-of-life symptoms.

Neither the blanket nor their closeness as they huddled together seemed to have much effect on this particular penetrating coldness nor did their lively conversation about anything and everything, except the football game, seem to bring any relief. A little warmth seemed to arrive in their laughter as Sue made the totally unexpected statement, "Right now, I would welcome a hot flash."

I suspect her sentiment could have been echoed throughout the football stadium, especially by our football team whose ability to score also seemed to be in a deep-freeze.

Who Is Putting Up With What?

Molline had lived in Winder previously but, several years before, had moved out of town. When she came into the office on a Saturday morning, my office staff greeted her warmly, as my old friend should be greeted.

After properly reciprocating the greeting, Molline remarked, "It is extremely important for me to see Doctor Skelton this morning. It could be a matter of life and death."

I had known Molline quite well before she moved out of town. She was considered to be stable and trustworthy, and had looked after my children and others as a long-term employee of our church nursery. Because she regarded her problem as urgent, she was quickly ushered into an examining room.

After giving my own personal greeting, I asked excitedly, "Molline, what is this urgent business that you desperately need to consult me about?"

She began, "Doctor, I'm worried about my sister, Corena. Corena is sure havin' a hard time and she won't talk to nobody about it! She has got her hands so much more than full.

"That man what she's married to…humph. He sho ain't nothing like the fine, nice, upstanding fellow what he's got you talked into thinkin' he is."

She had it right about my thinking her brother-in-law to be a fine, nice, upstanding fellow.

She continued her tirade, "Just because he owns a little farmland and makes his payments on time don't make him no gentleman. I can't prove it, but I believe his money comes from making moonshine likker.

"Shucks! He is just about as sorry as any one man could possibly be. Not only is he married to my sister and got them chillun by her, but on the other side of the county, somewhere out in them boondocks, he's got himself another wife. And he's got himself another bunch of chillun by her!"

My reply was, "I just can't see why Corena puts up with such stuff as that."

She answered quickly and emphatically, "Oh, it ain't her what's puttin' up with it. It's the other woman what's puttin' up with it. You see, he was married to her first!"

Molline never made me see the life and death possibility in this situation, but she filled a great void in my educational history when she helped me understand that "putting up with" something is strictly a matter of definition.

The Sheriff of Clacktown

Bill lived with his wife and family in a rural area of Barrow Country known as Clacktown, a vaguely defined area about eight or ten miles from Winder that entertains no thought of ever becoming incorporated. It is known by the family name of some long-term residents of the area. Bill's mother lived in the house next to him, about a hundred and fifty yards down the road.

Bill had previously suffered a severe heart attack and, after his recovery, had been advised to get plenty of rest and avoid excitement. On this particular day, he had worked harder than usual at the shop where he had long been employed and, being very tired, felt he needed and deserved a rest.

As he lay on his couch watching television, the telephone rang. Bill answered the phone and heard his mother saying frantically, "Bill, someone is trying to break into my house. I can hear them cutting the screen on the back door right now!"

Bill quickly jumped into his boots, without taking time to tie the strings. He grabbed his shotgun and bolted out the door, leaving the long boot-laces dangling.

As he exited the door onto his old-plantation style porch, he tried to make a 90 degree turn to the left towards the steps. However, he stepped on his trailing boot-string and could not move his leg in the direction of the needed turn. Instead, he fell headlong out the door and off of his four-foot-high porch onto the hard Georgia clay. The impact broke his collarbone and caused the shotgun to discharge making almost as much racket as his fall.

In great pain but still worried about his mother, Bill got to his feet and continued on his journey to his mother's home. When he got there, he found that indeed someone had begun to cut the screen to enter the house, but he saw no sign of them now. His spectacular exit from his own home had apparently frightened them enough to cause them to abandon their robbery attempt.

Nobody else seemed to see any humor in the situation when I saw Bill in the emergency room that night for treatment of his broken clavicle. However, as time wore on and Bill's lnjury healed, the situation seemed to be more generally regarded as being funny.

In spite of his unorthodox methods and harm to himself, you must admit…Bill got the job done.

Bill laughed many times with me about the incident and about his new title born in the emergency room that night. Until his sudden and untimely death a few years later, his well-earned title remained, "The Sheriff of Clacktown."

Soft Drinks Cause This?

Williamson and Heath were partners in a small country store, where they sold a fairly complete line of groceries, soft drinks and produce. More than anything else, they sold sweet cakes or crackers and soft drinks and they listened to or told some very tall tales as folks sat there communing.

No certified-for-real country store is complete and authentic without a full line of tall tales, regardless of how sparse or how full the line of merchandise may be.

Before the popularization of plastic money, Williamson and Heath specialized in an item the chain stores had long since abandoned…credit. Credit was the thing that allowed them to stay in business. They had to charge more than the chain stores to make up for their low volume. Ironically, it was probably credit that later put them out of business, since a high percentage of people would try to beat them at least once, and then would never come back. But, that has nothing whatsoever to do with this story.

One pathetic little girl, who appeared to be about 15 or 16 years old but had the mentality of one much younger, often came into the store to purchase small items for the family. Most of the time when she came in, she would buy a soft drink and drink it before she went home so she did not have to leave a deposit on the bottle. As fate would have it, this unfortunate young girl became pregnant out of wedlock.

When her family confronted her and asked about the pregnancy, she denied any wrongdoing. She persisted in this denial when asked on repeated occasions who had fathered the child. Instead, she always affirmed, "I ain't done nothing but go over to Mr. Williamson's and Mr. Heath's store and drink Pepsi Colas!"

In spite of her continued denials of any contact with the opposite sex or of any wrongdoing, her pregnancy advanced. As most pregnancies will, it eventually reached full term. She went into labor and came to our hospital where, as the doctor on call, I delivered a fine male child for her.

The baby was routinely housed in the newborn nursery, while the mother went to her room in the obstetrical wing of the hospital. Frankie, the nurses aide who attended the mother in the obstetrical wing, happened to live in the same general neighborhood as the patient, and bought a few things at the store.

Frankie knew of many of the factors in this case including the patient's statement about having done nothing except drink Pepsi at the store. She also knew Heath's real name was Tulliver. Furthermore, Frankie's duty required her to obtain all information from her patient including the new baby's name, and fill out the birth certificate.

Not surprisingly, the new mother did not have a name picked out for her child. After all, she had spent the entire pregnancy denying even the existence of a child, so she had not thought about what she might name her unwanted offspring. When she asked for Frankie's help in this matter, Frankie, obviously with tongue in cheek, suggested the name of William Tulliver.

The patient never suspected the significance of that name when she embraced it for her newborn son. But don't think for one-second the significance escaped Williamson and Heath, nor any of the tellers of tall tales who frequented their country store. For several weeks, and much to the chagrin of the two store owners, it served as the chief topic of conversation within the store.

My informants tell me the sale of Pepsi dropped significantly, especially among young girls in that community. I know for certain, until his death, any mention of Pepsi-Cola would bring a wry smile and soft curse from Williamson who enjoyed a good joke as much as anyone, even if he was the butt of it.

CHAPTER 8

HIGHS AND LOWS

*I*N MY OPINION, THE *practice of medicine should not be undertaken by anyone without a sense of being called by God to that high office, even as we expect our clergy to feel called. Whereas the clergy is pictured as standing between us and God in spiritual matters, the physician stands between us and God in emotional and physical matters. It is a position of great responsibility in which the stakes are often high. It can lead a practitioner to the highest of highs when success is achieved, and to the lowest of lows when failure is his lot.*

Contrary to the claims of some lawyers, medicine is far from an exact science. It if were an exact science, how could there be so much room for an advancement in even the central core of medicinal problems. How can it ever become exact when every patient has many variables and every problem is open to more than one point of view?

It has been my honor and privilege to serve one community in the position of family physician for more than 42 years. A full six years before that were spent in preparing for that service. In that much time, there have been many highs and some lows. Thank God, the high times have outnumbered the low ones. Lest my humorous stories leave the reader thinking I am flippant about the practice of medicine, I include here a few stories from the high/low group.

World Famous Teacher

My medical education came at Emory University whose Chairman of the Department of Medicine, Dr. Paul Beeson, would later be world famous as a professor. Dr. Beeson had surrounded himself with other excellent teachers, many of whom would become chairmen of medical departments in other schools around the world.

Dr. Beeson made the proper diagnosis in most cases, using the comparatively rudimentary methods available at the time. My diagnosis as a student often proved wrong on the same cases, but those are not the stories to be told at this time. The stories for now are about high points in my medical study years when my diagnosis proved correct even though it did not agree with the diagnosis of Dr. Beeson.

When my service assignment changed from Medicine to Surgery during my junior year, I inherited a young adult black male with severe abdominal pain, high spiking fever, low white blood-cell count and a generalized rash. He appeared seriously ill and, after several days, no general consensus existed as to his diagnosis.

Dr. Beeson suggested it might be, "Typhoid Fever with rose spots," a rare occurrence even in those days. Dr. Friedewald suggested "Infectious Mononucleosis with a rash," a condition not uncommonly encountered, but the patient seemed much too ill for that diagnosis.

In taking a new history on the patient, I stumbled onto the diagnosis by asking about the patient's experience with all childhood diseases individually, questions others had already asked in general fashion. My specific question that unlocked the mystery was, "Have you ever had measles?"

He answered, "No," and this led quickly to my next question, "Have you had any recent exposure to measles?"

Bingo! His nephew had broken out three weeks before his illness began, the exact time needed for incubation of measles. A quick look into *Cecil's Textbook of Medicine* showed appendicitis as a rare complication of measles. The pieces of the puzzle fell in place, and the patient had his ruptured appendix removed. He recovered after a stormy course.

A second high occurred the next year, when I inherited another patient at change of service. Her diagnosis had already been made and supposedly confirmed by x-rays. She presented as a very large, early middle-aged, black female with obvious, classical "Cushing's Syndrome," caused by too much of the adrenal hormone, Cortisone.

There are two different types of this syndrome. One is "Pituitary Cushing's" where the cause for the excess hormone is a tumor of the pituitary gland. The tumor sends excess stimulation to the adrenal glands resulting in excess Cortisone secretion and subsequent symptoms. The second is "Adrenal Cushing's," where the excess hormone comes from a primary tumor of one or both adrenal glands.

The patient's diagnosis, with which Dr. Beeson concurred, was listed as "Adrenal Cushing's Syndrome." she was scheduled for surgery for this serious condition within 72 hours after my arrival on the service.

My first glance at her raised doubts in my mind about the adrenal sub-diagnosis, because her eyes were severely crossed. The Pituitary gland is located inside the skull near the nerves that supply the eyes. The presence of tumor there can increase pressure on these nerves, paralyze an eye muscle and cause eyes to be crossed.

After our introductions, my first question to her was, "Have you always had crossed eyes?"

Her answer, "Not until about three years ago," did not surprise me in the least.

My next query sought to prove my point, "Do you have pictures from when your eyes were normal?"

She did have some pictures, but it took two days for these photos to be delivered to me. My, what a change they showed! No doubt existed in my mind, she had "Pituitary Cushing's Syndrome," and a note signed by me and stating that opinion with my reasons for it soon appeared on her chart.

A senior medical student's opinion that differs from that held by the Chairman of the Department of Medicine and the Chief Surgical Resident does not delay scheduled surgery. Taken as scheduled to the operating room, she died under induction of anesthesia. An autopsy revealed a cancerous tumor of the Pituitary gland.

No high was experienced from her death, but my correct diagnosis in the face of differing with the Chairman of the Department of Medicine did a world of good for my ego.

JIMSON WEED JUMPIES

September 1972, a time of year when every able bodied person on every farm in Louisiana was needed to harvest the precious cotton crop. Foolish as it appeared, this particular family left a six-year-old boy at home to care for his four-year-old sister. When the family returned from the fields just before dark, they were horrified to find the little girl in constant convulsions and the little boy mumbling and picking at imaginary creatures flying in the air. Both were completely incoherent.

When I saw the children in the emergency room, in addition to the above described symptoms, both had very rapid pulses, slightly elevated temperatures, extremely dry mouths and widely dilated pupils. These are all symptoms of poisoning with atropine or belladonna, but the family denied having any such medicines in the house. They could not give any helpful history.

In my reading only a few days earlier, a case report listed symptoms almost identical to those my patients exhibited. They reported on a child with stramonium intoxication from eating Jimson Weed plants, also called Thorn apple. The diagnosis, however, took several days to make since no modern toxicology panels were available at the time.

I was quite certain about the diagnosis with these two children, given their situation and symptoms and the similarity to the case reported in the article. They were admitted to the ward with the unequivocal diagnosis of "Stramonium Intoxication" and were begun on IV fluids and watchful care with only a minimum amount of light sedation to limit seizures.

The first thing next morning, when Dr. Gray, the hospital administrator, sent for me, I expected a commendation for a job well done.

"Skelton," he growled in an unexpectedly stern voice, "what do you mean by admitting a patient with a diagnosis like 'Stramonium Intoxication' and not even give consideration to other possibilities? I have practiced medicine for over 30 years, and have never even heard of such a case."

"Dr. Gray," I began my defense, "let me assure you that other diagnoses were considered, but there was reason to rule out each of them. The symptoms the children manifested were like those of atropine poisoning, yet no belladonna or atropine were in the house. I had recently read this article," I continued my argument and produced the article, "and these kids' symptoms were so similar to those in this article, I considered it a no-brainer. By the way, the Jimson Weed pods are maturing right now."

Dr. Gray remained dubious of my diagnosis until the little boy woke up later that day. When he was asked what they had done, his reply became my vindication. He shyly announced, "We et some of them burrs off of them trees."

In a couple of days, both children had recovered and gone home, and this first-year resident had gained considerable respect in the eyes of his boss.

The Only Case

The angry father brought his 16 year old son to my office. "Doc, I want you to see about my boy," said the father. "At football practice yesterday, he tackled this boy so hard, he busted his helmet. Ever since then, he's had this terrible headache. I called the school, and they told me they ain't got no insurance. I reckon I'm gonna have to pay you myself."

Examination showed him to have a temperature of 101F, an unexpected finding in a head injury in which the patient is still conscious. His pupils were equal and reactive but he did have a slightly stiff neck. My mind swept back to the words of Dr. Beeson, "If a patient has a headache and a fever, think about Weil's Disease."

A complete history and physical examination shed no further light on his situation. A spinal tap showed a mild increase in the white cell count, consistent with Weil's Disease.

Weil's Disease is quite uncommon. The source of infection is usually unknown. Its official name is "Leptospirosis Icterohemorrhagicum," signifies its cause (an uncommonly found spiral type of bacteria known as Leptospira), and its symptoms in more advanced stages (the white portion of the eyes, of critically ill patients often show yellow color, or "icterus," and hemorrhage, producing a picture of reddish-yellow eyeballs).

My total experience with the disease had been gained in a single case treated during my internship, a black female whose disease had already reached advanced stages before her admission. She had died.

The greatest problem in diagnosing "Weil's Disease in that era was that no immediate test could prove or disprove the diagnosis. Unless you were fortunate enough to actually visualize one of these rare corkscrew-like bacteria under the microscope, you had to rely on serological titers for the diagnosis. Serological titers took two or more weeks to complete, and your patient either died or got well before the diagnosis was certain.

We looked in his urine for Leptospira, ordered a blood sample for Weil's Disease titer and put the patient on IV fluids along with high doses of the antibiotic of choice, my memory says penicillin. He improved rapidly. After his discharge from the hospital, a second blood sample was drawn for a two-week serological titer for Weil's Disease.

A few days late, a team of epidemiologists from the Georgia Department of Public Health covered the entire hill where the boy lived. The titers had shown proof of Weil's Disease. They took blood from every member of his family, his closest friends and every neighborhood dog and hog they could catch. None showed evidence of the disease. Public health officials speculated he caught it from swimming in a pasture pond—whose dam had broken during his hospital stay in a rainstorm.

For the boy, his family and for myself, I felt a sense of great elation. That no other case of Weil's Disease has been reported in Barrow County before or since, still gives me a sense of pride.

Ecstasy And Agony

My eyes were drawn to the little boy held in his mother's arms near the entrance to the emergency room. He had telltale signs of Waterhouse-Friedrickson Syndrome, a universally fatal disease if not treated aggressively within a few minutes—or hours at the most. Neither the child or his mother was familiar to me, but we had no time to waste.

Waterhouse-Friedrickson Syndrome is a condition in which Meningococci, bacteria that cause classical meningitis, get into the bloodstream in massive quantities. It causes multiple hemorrhages throughout the body, giving the patient a widely scattered purplish rash, characteristic of the disease. This rash formed the basis for my hasty diagnosis. The adrenal glands are virtually wiped out by these hemorrhages and the body is deprived of its life supporting cortisones. Unless these hormones are quickly supplied artificially in large quantities, the patient does not survive.

Although he had never been my patient, I directed the nurse to take the child immediately into the treatment room. An IV was established, a blood culture drawn and large doses of antibiotics and cortisone were begun. After his admission to an isolation room, we kept him under very close observation with blood pressure checks every five or ten minutes. If his pressure dropped below a certain point, more cortisone was given.

No exact treatment protocol had been established for these cases, so we had to react to his reactions. As the old military pilots say, "We had to fly by the seat of our britches." Cortisone blood levels could not be determined at the time, so laboratory treatment guides were essentially not available. The blood culture did grow Meningococcus, and we became even more certain of the correctness of the diagnosis.

Transfer to another hospital could not be considered because of the need for constant observation and reaction. Our greatest fear was that we would lose touch with the patient at a critical time, in that era before mobile phone and reliable long-range radios.

Remarkably, the boy survived those first few critical hours as we followed our ever-changing battle plan. Hours became days, and he showed signs of actual improvement. Knowing the dangers of excessive cortisone, we decreased his dose slightly. When this produced no adverse reaction, we lowered it again. In stepwise fashion over several days, we completely stopped his cortisone dosage and the patient remained stable and appeared no worse for the change.

The battle had been won, even though the odds against his recovery had been incredibly large. Our whole treatment team was ecstatic.

The patient's family members were exceedingly grateful and had many kind things to say about the way their son had been snatched from the jaws of death by our aggressive handling of his illness. The whole family became my patients, and did more than any previous group had done to spread my name throughout the region. They held me in high esteem.

Possibly a year had elapsed when they brought a younger child, a little girl, to my office. Beautiful in her appearance, she had the round face and rosy cheeks usually associated with the best of health.

This child had an enlarged lymph gland in the front portion of her neck that did not appear red, nor did it seem particularly tender. It felt relatively soft—certainly not the stony hard consistency sometimes associated with the dreaded cancer. Her family gave no history of known fever or night-sweats.

No elevation showed in her white blood-cell count, and in no area of her slightly chubby body could be found any other evidence of enlarged nodes. Her spleen did not seem enlarged, so we felt reasonably comfortable in assuring the family she did not have a form of leukemia or lymphoma.

Except for the enlarged lymph gland, no other positive physical finding showed except moderate decay in her baby teeth, which had not been completely shed at the time. Assuming the drainage from her infected teeth to be the cause of the enlarged node, we began the patient on a sulfa drug and advised the family to use hot compresses to the area three or four times a day. The child would be seen again in two weeks if the node had not cleared by that time. No doubt existed in my mind she would respond well and not require another visit.

To my chagrin and amazement, however, she had to be seen again and the node had not seemed to change in the least. On this visit, we prescribed a form of Penicillin by mouth and scheduled another office visit. Surely, this drug will solve our problem, I thought as she left my office.

On the third visit, if any change was noted, it had to be slight enlargement of the gland and a suggestion of pus formation in the mass. The failure of both Sulfa and Penicillin seemed almost unbelievable to me, but we still had the remaining option of Tetracycline, an expensive, new, broad-spectrum antibiotic that would almost certainly produce a cure. We prescribed Tetracycline and requested a return visit.

On the return visit, there had still been no improvement. Almost two months had been spent in treatment, with no improvement noted. Totally frustrated I discussed our treatment options with the family. It appeared to me, we had to know exactly what we were dealing with and the only option left was to biopsy the mass. Surgical biopsy appeared to be the best procedure available at this time before techniques for needle biopsy had been developed.

Surgical biopsy is not a difficult technique to master. I had done it many times before, most often under local anesthesia. To attempt this procedure on the neck of a young child using only local anesthesia appeared possibly quite dangerous and somewhat callous. In our opinion, it would be much more safe and humane to use a general anesthetic in this situation.

Her scheduled surgery was nearly complete when she suddenly turned extremely blue and her heart quit beating. Closed-chest heart message had not been described at this time, but a few patients had been salvaged by opening the chest to massage her heart. As we prepared to open her chest, the heart regained its rhythm, but the damage had been done. She was brought from the operating room with unmistakable signs of irreversible brain damage.

My devastation equaled that of her family. I was depressed to the point of being physically ill and unable to personally care for her needs in the few remaining hours of her life. Her family's hurt and anger had to be understood. In their opinion, I, who before this time had been so great, had not only killed their daughter but had abandoned her in her last hours of life. It remains the most difficult cross I ever bore.

After her death, I re-treated that child thousand of times in my mind and never saw another option for her treatment. My grief for her lasted at least two years. Forty-plus years later, it still hurts to think about or write about her unfortunate death. With this one family came probably the highest and the lowest points of my medical career.

[Author's Note:] The pathology report came back us "Scrofula," an infection with Tuberculosis in the lymph nodes in the neck. It was a possibly curable disease with the use of a relatively dangerous drug called Streptomycin, if we had only known.

Measles Manufactured Mayhem

The child had obvious measles but with marked stiffness in her neck. In spite of all our efforts to control it, her temperature rose higher than our thermometers could register before we were able to bring it down by using extreme measure like ice-water baths and ice-water enemas. It required no degree of genius to determine the child had Measles Encephalitis, the most dreaded of many complications of this childhood disease.

Sparse reports were in the medical literature of children spared the most disastrous results of this complication by the administration of large doses of serum immune globulin. We ordered it for her. The order also included having the medication delivered by the Louisiana State Patrol, since we knew the hospital would not have nearly the needed amount of this modern medical marvel already on hand.

Much to my chagrin, the head of procurement for the hospital refused the order on the basis of its expense. My red face denoted my anger as we confronted one another and he defended his position, "I can fund the entire hospital stay of two or three patients with what this one medicine would cost, and there is no guarantee of its success."

"Yes, but if it is successful, she will be saved and the State of Louisiana may be spared the lifetime burden of another welfare case."

As he obstinately held his position, my anger grew even greater. "The idea…putting money before a human life." I blurted out as I found myself scaling over the counter separating us.

The opened pocket knife in his hand looked mighty large to me as I regained my balance on his side of the counter.

In the armed forces, I had trained troops to disarm a person with a knife or bayonet, so I had no great fear of his weapon. My Army lectures had also included a statement, "If there is any way to avoid hand-to-hand combat, then take it," This seemed certainly to be the time to look for an alternate way.

I begged, "My job is to save lives. Yours is to save money for the State. You know I have never wasted one dime of the State's money, and I believe we have a chance here to save a lot of it in the long run. Why don't you give in to me this time and let's try to save this little girl's life. There's no need for either one of us to get hurt over it."

"You know, you may be right," he agreed. Before dark that night, the medicine had been delivered and administered. He and I shook hands and remained the best of friends from that time on.

My keen disappointment showed the nest morning when the little girl greeted me with a decerebrate cry, a certain sign she had permanent brain damage. She left the hospital showing no sign of mental recovery, and I suppose there will always be the question in my mind, "Would she have been better off had we not fought so hard for the medication which may have saved her life, but not have saved her brain function?"

CHAPTER 9

NORTH GEORGIA SWEET POTATO

*W*HEN THE CB RADIO *fad swept the nation and before its language became vile and vulgar as it is now, I bought two run-of-the-mill units and placed one in my automobile and another in my boat. Then, there began a search for a suitable "handle" so this novice could properly speak the CB lingo.*

In our search, we went through several handles having to do with my profession, my love for fishing, my coarse short red hair, and many others, but nothing seemed to fit.

Then Nora, my wife, suggested the handle of "Sweet Potato," and gave the following reasons:

> *You are always telling those stories about sweet potatoes.*
>
> *When you try, you can be a right sweet potato yourself.*

So my handle became "North Georgia Sweet Potato," but that is of no interest to you unless you know the stories behind the title. One story relates to my childhood, a second involved my father and the third is about a patient who was going to have a baby. But, I am getting ahead of myself. Let me tell you those sweet potato stories:

Beef Heart?

My father worked as a streetcar conductor in Atlanta before, during and after the great depression. The street car-line he worked at the time of this story ended in one of the black sections of Atlanta. During this time of legal segregation, black people in the South were required to sit in the back seats on public transportation. It seemed peculiar to me that, at the end of the line when the electric trolleys and the seat backs were reversed, the back of the streetcar now became the front and the front became the back. After the change, a black person was not allowed to sit where he was required to sit before.

Because of extreme economic conditions in the South, people learned not to waste anything and would eat every part of any animal they killed, including the intestines (called chitterlings or Chit'lin's) and the heart.

One day as Daddy sat waiting for the scheduled time to begin his run back into Atlanta, there sat only one passenger on the streetcar, a black man dutifully located in one of the rear seats. A second black man boarded through the open front door of the waiting streetcar. He was eating a large baked sweet potato.

The first passenger called to the newcomer, "Hey, fellah, wha's that you're eatin,' beef heart?"

His friend's reply was to-the-point, "Naw, it'll be faht tomorrow." *You know, he was probably right.*

Just A Starving Boy

Throughout my childhood and even into adulthood, my ravenous appetite remained a source of embarrassment to me. I would often eat until nausea overcame me, excuse myself from the group to regurgitate, then go back to eat more. This stomach purging occurred as the organ's natural way of rebelling against intense overstuffed pressure, never from any self-induction.

My hatred of myself for this gluttony became intense, but I seemed powerless to do anything about it. In those days, no one considered it an illness. The person afflicted in that way was just considered a "hog." Naturally, a lot of teasing by those who knew about my problem came along with the affliction.

General policy in every public and private school of that day required assembly of all students each and every day. This assembly bore the title of "Chapel" and required every student to be in attendance. Because of the frequency of holding Chapel, good programs seemed in short supply, and most of the programs had little substance. The principal had to rely on his own ingenuity to fill chapel time and he also had to teach classes.

I must have been in the fifth grade when our principal, Mr. Allison, stood before the entire school body and reported, "I was coming around the corner of the school building today when I heard somebody crying. It seemed to be coming from behind the shrubbery. I walked back there to look, and there between the shrubbery and the building, I saw Red Skelton."

When he said that, my ears really pricked up. Mr. Allison was not only my principal but also a teacher and a Baptist preacher, and he appeared ready to tell a lie. In fact, he already had told one, because what he had said before the whole student body had simply never happened.

Mr. Allison continued, "I asked, 'Red, what in the world is the matter with you?'

"Red looked up at me with tears dripping off his chin, and said, 'Mr. Allison, somebody has done stolen every dab of my lunch except for just 13 baked sweet potatoes.'"

Even though his story was untrue and hit me where it hurt, I had to laugh.

On further pondering of the matter, my conviction grew that whoever stole my lunch must have been merciless to leave a growing boy with no more to eat than 13 sweet potatoes. No wonder my tears were flowing when Mr. Allison found me.

His Name is "Tater"

[Author's Note:] To understand the following story, many readers will need explanation as to the planting of sweet potatoes, often just called "taters" in the South. When a farmer plans to plant sweet potatoes, he must first prepare an area of finely pulverized dirt and mulch called a bed. He then puts whole sweet potatoes in this bed and lightly covers them with dirt, mulch and straw. With watering, the green sprouts of sweet potatoes soon appear, many sprouts from each potato. These young sprouts are pulled from the bed and gathered for planting. Once they are gathered, they are called "potato slips" or simply "slips." These slips are then planted in rows in the field and from their roots come sweet potatoes.

Margo had one previous child, who had just celebrated his nineteenth birthday. Imagine her surprise when, on a visit to my office, she received the news that her 'change-of-life problem" actually came from a pregnancy.

When the shock was over and Margo came back to the office for a visit, I asked her, "What do you plan to name this baby?"

Margo replied hesitantly, "Well, Doctor Skelton, I reckon I'll have to name him 'Tater,' 'cause he shore come from a slip."

Many times I wondered where Snuffy Smith and Loweezy of the comic strip had gotten the name "Tater," for their child. My assumption is that Margo told me. It's surprising what kind of education you can get from your patients.

CHAPTER 10

OH! THOSE KIDNEY STONES!

Of all the painful ailments that attack men, the most painful may well be an attack of kidney colic, as a stone from the kidney tries to pass through a small tube called the ureter and make its way to the bladder. Thank God, this problem has never happened to me, but I have seen men larger and stronger than myself literally roll on the floor with pain.

It has always been interesting to me to hear the reaction of the patient's wife. More often than not, her response is not one of great sympathy. She is likely to say something like, "Well, he finally knows how I felt those times when I had labor pains."

Women who have experienced both tell me the pain from kidney stones is as close as a man can come to knowing the pain a woman feels during labor. In my experience, no man who has ever suffered the pain of a kidney stone would be willing to belittle his wife's labor pains.

Even though it might seem an unlikely time to find any humor, very funny things often happen at times of great pain. It appears to me that one had just as well laugh as cry and the Good Book does say, "A merry heart doeth good like a medicine." {Prov. 7:22}

Let me share a couple of my kidney stone stories:

Testimony Of My Good Looks

Red had a kidney stone and suffered its terrific pain. His wife called and asked me to come to their house to treat him. However, with a patient in hard labor at that moment who I expected to deliver at any minute, it seemed too risky for me to leave right then. They could find no other doctor available and Red's wife said she could not possibly get him to the emergency room. That meant he had to wait until I could get free before he could get any relief.

Red paced the floor—that did not help.

He tried heat, then ice—that did not help.

He went to bed and got into every imaginable position—none of these helped, either.

He cried. Even that did not help.

Finally, with the delivery of the baby completed, the house call could be made. Red looked happily at this ugly countenance of mine and exulted, "You look better to me then any movie star."

Surely, beauty is in the mind and the eye of the beholder.

A Drink Out Of My Bottle

Robert, a black patient well known for his love of liquor, had been my patient for years. Almost every time you saw him, you found him either drinking or already drunk. Drinking caused Robert to be more funny than usual but, whether sober or drunk, he mortally feared a shot needle.

On one occasion, Robert's family called me to see him because of severe pain in his abdomen and back. When I got to his home, he rolled constantly in the bed with exceedingly severe pain due to a kidney stone. His pain was too severe to be relieved by any medications by mouth, and he must have a shot of Morphine.

With the shot readied, I had to chase Robert all over the bed to give it to him. I persisted and won the battle. Now, duty required me to stay long enough to be certain the medicine did its work, fighting with impatience every second of my wait to see if he got any relief.

As he seemed to be getting a little drowsy, I raised the question, "Robert, you are an authority on drunks. Tell me, what do you think of my kind of drunk?"

A little drowsy, he replied, "Doctor, yo' drunk is fine, but yo' bottle's jes' too hard to drink out of."

OLD HAMMOND

Elsa, in her mid-seventies showed great diligence in caring for her son, Hammond, in his mid-fifties. Hammond remained seriously ill, with much damage to both kidneys brought about by a huge stone in each. He had overwhelming infection, much pus in the urine and a high fever. He also had uremia, a condition most lay people call "kidney poisoning," caused by poor kidney function. Dialysis had not been developed and kidney transplant was in its infancy in that day. Discussion had been held about a transplant, but no donor system was available.

Dr. Graves and I were conferring in a hospital hallway one day, when Elsa quite brusquely interrupted us to speak about her son. "Doctors," she said, "I want to talk to you about old Hammond." (Those were her exact words "Old Hammond.")

"Old Hammond is in really bad shape, ain't he?" she continued. "What with them old stones in both kidneys and all that pus and fever and that old kidney-poisoning…Tell me, doctors, do you reckon old Hammond is a'gonna' croak?"

[Author's Note:] For any who are interested, "Old Hammond" did not croak, at least not on this admission. He improved a great deal with the treatment and he, later, moved to Florida where efforts were still unsuccessful to obtain the kidney donor he needed. I am told Hammond died several years later in another state.

CHAPTER 11

THE TITLEHOLDER

Sam Boon coveted the title of Barrow County's greatest liar. It seemed he sought that title constantly with the persistence of a prizefighter going after the world heavy-weight crown. In my humble opinion, he won the title hands down.

Rosie, his wife, did her part by accepting everything Sam said at less than face value by tolerating the fairly large number of fishermen who made the trek to her back porch. When they lifted her freezer lid, she knew someone had fallen victim to a favorite of Sam's tall tales. To wit;

"Man, I sure did catch a big bass yesterday. That thing weighed 16-and-a-half pounds. If you don't believe me, just go to my house and lift up the lid on that old freezer chest on my back porch. She's laying on top waiting to be mounted. Boy, she did put up a fight, I never thought I'd get her landed as big as she was and me with no landing-net—especially when she got hung up in that bush."

Every guy taken in by that story felt like a fool until he found out what elite company he kept. Sam made it sound so real, many of Barrow County's finest had fallen for the tale. Would you pass up an opportunity to see such a whopper in the largemouth-bass species, if you were a fisherman? Well, you would soon find the real largemouth to be Sam Boon.

No Time To Lie

To my knowledge, there was only one wrecker in all of Barrow County when I arrived in Winder. There seems to be one on nearly every street corner now. In those early days before increased traffic, there were few calls even for the one wrecker here; but when a call did come, there would occasionally be more than one vehicle involved in the accident and needing to be removed from the highway.

Because he loved hunting and fishing and spent as much time in the woods as he possibly could, Sam had an old Jeep with a small winch mounted on its front bumper, an unwieldy, mechanical, thing that geared somehow to his Jeep's motor. He used it mostly to pull his own vehicle out of the mud when it got stuck in the woods of the wild areas he hunted or fished. But sometimes, Sam would get a call from law-enforcement agents to pull a disabled vehicle out of the road so traffic could pass when more than one vehicle got disabled in an accident.

One day after Sam had completed his work as a carpenter, he came home and saw visitors sitting on his porch in conversation with Rosie. Actually, they were more likely just listening to Rosie, something Sam rarely did.

Apparently, these visitors knew Sam fairly well because the man called out even before he had gotten out of his Jeep, "Come on in, Sam, and tell us a lie."

"I ain't got time," Sam replied with a grin and without a moment of hesitation. He didn't even cut off his ignition switch or get out of his Jeep.

"They just called me from the Barrow County Sheriff's Department," he yelled. "There's been a bad wreck down on the

Monroe Highway and they need me and this front-end winch to pull out one of the cars that are blocking the highway."

Having said that, he scratched gravel with his rear wheels as he sped out of the driveway in the direction of the Monroe Highway. As soon as he drove out of sight, Sam pulled into the first side street and hid to watch his visitors as they sped by on their way to see the terrible accident on the Monroe Highway.

But he did not have time to tell them a lie.

Two Windmills

Sam Boon claimed that, in his childhood, he and his father were worried about the high cost of electricity and decided to do something about it. According to their figures, it would take two small windmills to do the job. Working together, they designed and built every part of those two windmills. After the windmills were assembled and put in place on top of their highest hill, to their great dismay, neither of them would work.

"So, we took both of 'em down and examined each one of 'em piece-by-piece," Sam continued. "Every piece was perfect, so we put 'em both back up again.

"You know, them things still wouldn't work and neither one of us could see a single reason why they wouldn't.

"But we finally did figure out what was wrong.

"We had to take one of 'em down. We just didn't have enough wind on that hilltop to blow both of 'em."

Doesn't that sound reasonable to you?

Camping Out

As he campaigned for the title of Barrow County's greatest liar, Sam Boon told this story:

"Me and Rosie went on a vacation together." That by itself seemed a pretty good tale because you rarely saw the two of them together away from their home.

"We rented a little cabin up in North Georgia and it looked like she wanted to take everything we owned. She carried so much stuff, we had to go in a two-ton truck. When we got all that stuff in the cabin, it filled it plumb full from front-to-back and bottom-to-top. You couldn't put nothing else anywhere in there.

"Then, that woman remembered she hadn't brought along anything to make us any biscuits. She sent me to the store to get a 25-pound sack of flour.

"When I got back with that sack of flour," Sam rambled on, "I couldn't get it into that cabin nowhere. There wasn't no room! I had to take that sack and hang it on a big old nail out on the front porch.

"That night, just after midnight, there come a great big windstorm up in them mountains. It blew so confounded strong… would you believe, it blew the sack right off that flour but it left every bit of the flour a'hanging on the nail."

A Trash-Moving Rain

A group of Winder men standing around shooting the bull after a meeting were discussing a heavy rainstorm and referred to it as a "trash-moving rain." Sam Boon walked up and heard the tail end of their conversation.

"Shucks," he said, "ain't none of you fellows ever seen a real trash-moving rain. They just don't seem to happen no more but, when I was a boy, I seen one.

"My Grandpa run a little mill on the Toccoa River, and he ground corn and wheat. He built his waterwheel in the middle of the stream bed below his dam and almost parallel to it. Then, he built a run-around that took the water through a wooden chute headin' back towards the middle, where it dumped over the water wheel.

"One summer, I was a'helpin' him, and we was a'grindin' corn. All of a sudden, it seemed to come out of nowhere…the darnedest rain you ever seen. I mean a sure enough gully washer…a real trash-mover. That river rose up the quickest you could imagine and the water run right over the middle of the dam.

"When the water got to running over the dam, it hit the mill-wheel on the back side and started turning it backward. Before we could get it stopped, it had done put 40 bushels of meal right back on the cob."

My agreement with Sam is complete. That qualifies as a trash-moving rain.

Sam Boon Goes Fishing With Me

One summer, Sam Boon and I went with the local troop of Boy Scouts, for a wild week of wilderness camping in the Okeefenokee Swamp. Fortunately, other adults were along who were bona fide Scout leaders. Sam and myself were just along as sponsors and had never qualified for a leader's role.

My gear for this trip included a small trotline with 35 hooks on it and, for bait, some shrimp that had previously been thawed and refrozen more than once. It was raunchy!

You can imagine my surprise when we returned to camp the first evening and discovered those shrimp had been cooked for our dinner by the scout leader, without even peeling them. They were completely inedible for humans, and even those ravenous coons that inhabit Billy's Island in the swamp and will eat anything, turned up their noses when they were discarded.

Refusing to give up the idea of using his trotline, this fisherman got in his car and, after a round-trip of 70+ miles, located some pork liver, the only available bait commonly used for trotlines.

There being only a limited quantity available the entire supply was purchased and brought back to camp.

Next morning as we embarked on our swamp exploration, the trotline lay in my tackle box and the liver in my cooler. Just before our return to camp that evening, the trotline was brought out, each hook baited with liver, and the entire contraption submerged.

After supper, when I told the crew I was going to go check the trotline, Sam Boon said, "I think I'll go with you."

We got into the boat and went to the spot where the trotline lay submerged. To my surprise, it seemed to be alive with catfish.

We worked the entire trotline, taking off all the fish and re-baiting each hook with liver. Twelve catfish were taken off the line, but when we reached the last hook, it still jumped with more fish.

So we worked the line a second time and took off five more catfish. Amazingly, it still jangled with fish and, with excitement growing with every fish removed, we worked the line a third time. This time we removed three catfish.

After working the line three times, it showed no further activity and I sat in the boat musing about my best luck ever when using a trotline. It seemed almost like the old fisherman's story of having to hide behind a tree to bait his hook.

As my eyes focused on Sam Boon, the realization hit me. "I'll be darned!" I bemoaned. "Here I am having the best luck I have ever had with a trotline, and who do I have to confirm my story but Sam Boon, the biggest liar in Barrow County."

But that bunch of fish spoke for themselves.

CHAPTER 12

More Outlandish Tales

The Original Purpose

OVER THE YEARS, MANY people had complained about the size of my finger used for examining the prostate gland. To examine this gland, a person must insert a gloved finger into the patient's rectum and simply feel the gland's size, determine its consistency and note any areas of tenderness or any nodules.

Since nothing could be done about the size of my finger, I always used a large amount of lubricating jelly to make its insertion a little less obtrusive. On completion of the examination, the patient would be handed a box of facial tissues to be used for removal of excess jelly.

On one occasion, a young man came into the office who had fairly severe pain in the lower abdomen and back. He had a low-grade fever and some difficulty with urination. I suspected inflammation of his prostate gland and a detailed examination was performed to determine the cause of his pain.

On completion of the examination, we placed a box of Kleenex type tissues before the patient, as per our routine. He lifted one or two tissues out of the box, blew his nose, pulled up his trousers and went home.

After all, everyone knows the original purpose for Kleenex was for nose-blowing, and it has been its purpose for more than 60 years.

A Commercial Venture?

The 30 year old female patient complained of mild to moderate pain in her abdomen for several days. She had nausea without vomiting and a severe loss of appetite. No burning or pain on urination and no evidence of blood in the urine were noted. Examination of her urine specimen was normal. Physical examination showed no temperature elevation and was essentially not remarkable except for considerably tenderness in the lower abdomen. There were no signs of peritonitis.

Her diagnosis could not be made on these limited findings, so I asked Eunice, my capable, long-term office attendant, to ready my patient for an examination of the pelvic organs. I left the room. Eunice assisted the patient to get ready for the examination and draped the area properly. Then, she also left the room.

What occurred in our absence is a matter of conjecture, but apparently, our patient feared there might have been some excessive moisture in that area. Our theory is, she took a facial tissue from her pocketbook to dry the area while we were absent from the room.

I quickly dismissed from my mind any idea it might be advertising or any form of commercial venture when I saw perfectly poised on her pubic prominence an S & H Green Stamp.

Her examination was completed in a professional manner without a word being spoken. I couldn't talk. I was biting my tongue.

Gretel And Tolbert

Gretel, a fun loving, petite, redheaded extrovert who nearly always saw the bright side of things loved to be in a crowd. She did not shun being the center of attention, although she did not always seek it. Gretel appreciated her friends and had plenty of them because she listened attentively to what other people said. Most of the time, she saw humor in every situation and enjoyed having a good laugh, and her hearty laughter lifted your: spirits. She also was capable of giving helpful advice when needed.

A great practical joker, she loved to draw from her own large collection of humor in telling funny stories or jokes. When Gretel told a tale, she usually drew the total attention of everyone in the crowd because she was good at it.

She could make an earthworm laugh.

Her husband, Tolbert, was an entirely different situation, being a worrier by nature and a confirmed, introverted workaholic. Naturally quite small of stature, Tolbert probably never weighed more than one-hundred-and-ten pounds. I really don't remember having ever heard him laugh, but Gretel declared I judged him too harshly.

He never told me a joke or a funny story. In his defense, most of the time when we were together, someone he loved was ill and this always gave him cause to worry. He did not need much cause to set him off in that direction. Tolbert certainly never sought the spotlight.

Gretel and Tolbert seemed to be extremely happy together and were still obviously in love, even after the multiple trials of parenting three children. Given the marked difference in their personalities, I wondered how these two became husband and wife, regardless of how they appeared.

Many years before Tolbert's sudden death from a massive heart attack, I uneasily asked Gretel, "How did you and Tolbert ever get together…I mean…to get married?"

Her reply really caught me off base when she stated, "Well, Dr. Skelton, when I was a young girl, I got real sick. I went to my doctor and, after he checked me over, he told me to go home and put something light on my stomach.

"I thought it over real good and Tolbert seemed to be about the lightest thing I could think of—so that's how we came to get married."

My suspicions were confirmed. A good and logical reason did indeed exist for this union.

Aunt Mable

Aunt Mable graduated from nursing school in the post-depression era of the mid-1930's, and soon became one of the pioneer public-health nurses in Georgia.

Before my enrollment in medical school, Aunt Mable discretely left me out of her medical conversations. After I became a student of medicine and, therefore a confederate who could be party to her knowledge and her stories, she allowed me to be privy to the following story:

The effects of the depression were still much in evidence and poverty was the rule, not the exception. A hopelessly backward, wretchedly poor county in South Georgia became the place where Aunt Mable began her career. She had never before seen such conditions, nor even dreamed they existed. With her heart feeling like it would break, she entered into her work of trying to help these suffering people with great gusto.

"One of the greatest problems with which I had to deal was the high birth rate," bemoaned Aunt Mable. "These poor folks did not have electric blankets to keep them warm at night nor television to keep them entertained. They all seemed to find the same way to keep themselves warm and entertained, and it seemed a new baby came into each household almost every year."

"With the family budget already strained beyond endurance, the birth of a new baby was a severe blow to the family economy. Though they rarely failed to love these babies, the family was hard pressed to adequately care for them. Many became malnourished and some of them soon succumbed to disease and/or starvation," she decried in her best medical jargon.

"The Public Health Department," in my opinion somewhat secretly in those days, "had a supply of crude, early prototype contraceptive devices. The device, a small, loosely woven, cloth bag with a string attached, contained some type of chemical designed to kill sperm.

"In theory, the woman should insert the moistened, chemical-laden bag before any sex contact. The chemicals would mix with both the male and female secretions to kill most of the sperm, thus reducing the likelihood of pregnancy," she continued in businesslike fashion.

Being keenly aware of the great problem of too-large families in her county, Aunt Mable obtained a supply of these contraceptive gadgets. She began to issue them to families where she considered the need to be really urgent. To her great surprise, the idea and the gadgets were accepted quite well by these rural folk.

"I thought these contraceptives might be helping us some in our fight," she continued, "but the solution of the problem continued to be only partial because of a lack of understanding on the part of the patients. With no scientific background, they simply could not fathom how such a thing could work nor how to use them properly.

"I especially remember one poor woman who had far too many children. This poor soul came into the clinic for a checkup after delivery of a child. I seized the opportunity to use this wonderful new agent, and gave her a supply of the devices with explicit, clearly worded directions as to how they should be used.

"I also instructed her, when these are gone, feel free to come back. I will be happy to give you some more. If you continue to use these every time you and your husband have sex, you won't ever have to be pregnant again, unless that is what you really want to happen."

Certain that she had made her point and rejoicing in one more victory over an unwanted pregnancy, Aunt Mable discharged the lady from the clinic.

Alas! The next time she saw that patient was in the obstetrical clinic—pregnant again, for the umpteenth time.

With great disappointment, Aunt Mable exclaimed, "I thought I told you to come back and get some more of those gadgets when you ran out!"

"Yessum, you did," said the extremely contrite patient, "but when I give out, our old truck was broke down and I didn't have no way to git here. Besides, I don't drive and it looks like my old man jes' has to work ever' hour of work he can possibly git jes' fer us to barely live."

"So, when those give out, I jes' knitted me some!"

Wouldn't you expect that to be a beautiful child after being strained through a sachet bag? Also, one is left to wonder how this mother ever did any household chores with so much knitting to do.

B-Bomb's Big Boo-Boo

After Aunt Mable's death, plans were made for her funeral. We placed a call to Smith's Memory Chapel, operated by B-Bomb Smith, and had her body removed to his establishment. Her funeral must be held in a celebration manner at her beloved First Baptist Church of Winder. Her will called for her to be buried beside her husband in their family plot in College Park, just outside Atlanta. The funeral director assured us he had everything under control and knew exactly how to get to the cemetery.

After the funeral, about 20 cars were in the procession for the 45 mile drive to the cemetery. B-Bomb drove the lead car, with the preacher riding with him

Things went well until we neared the I-285 junction with I-85 and saw much evidence of road construction. Directional signs were confusing, and B-Bomb became uncertain of our location. A short distance after entering I-85, he pulled off at an exit.

Aunt Mable's only nephew, Eddie, drove one of the lead cars in the procession and he knew the area like he knew the back of his hand. He agreed to take the lead and guide us to the cemetery.

When you pull 20 cars off the expressway at an exit, there is no way for the convoy to reenter that express corridor without much danger. Eddie recognized this danger and took the only safe route available from our present location.

Our funeral procession went right through the busiest airport in the world. We bounced over the speed bumps in front of the South Terminal, bumps placed there to slow down traffic for pedestrians going to board their planes. We took a rather circuitous route over side streets, before we finally arrived at the cemetery.

I am told our preacher became greatly embarrassed by this turn of events and suggested he might lie down in the floorboard of the hearse so no one could see him. Never will you drag out of me B-Bomb's reputed response to the preacher.

It is my opinion that a smiling and happy Aunt Mable gave a celestial thumbs-up to the spectacular and humorous exit of her body to her final resting place.

I still smile at the thought.

Another Crisis

[Author's Note:] The following incident occurred when the crisis in Beirut, Lebanon, reached its height and the U.S. had troops there as a peacekeeping force for the United Nations.

Pauline, an extremely nice, calm, mild-mannered lady, looked to be nearly middle-aged. Her public image appeared so mild, she would make Casper Milquetoast seem like a villain. She had married young and came from the school that believes a husband is truly head of the household. You would never expect any type of manipulation of her husband by this lady.

Brady, Pauline's husband, may be slightly older. A confirmed workaholic, Brady seemed convinced the only thing worse than missing a day of work would be to have to go to the doctor. His philosophy appeared to be, "If we can just give it a little more time, it will heal by itself." He was so tough, he considered it a sign of weakness to ever give in to your pain. Perhaps that's why he had such a difficult time when he had a heart attack later in life.

Under normal conditions, it practically required an armed escort to get Brady to the doctor's office, and I somehow got the impression he might have been hardheaded. So you can imagine my surprise when I saw Brady in my office completely unattended.

Seeing a look of great pain on his face, I asked, "What is the matter today, old buddy?"

"Doc," he replied, "it's my shoulder. Man, that thing's just killing me day and night!"

"How long has it hurt you?" I asked.

This time, Brady's answer came with a little chuckle, "About two weeks…but it ain't been so bad except the last three or four days. I can't even lift the thing at all, and at work, I've been just having to show the other men how to do it. I ain't been able to do one thing.

"And, Doc, I ain't been able to sleep. For the last three nights, I don't think I even closed my eyes, that thing hurt me so bad. I didn't let my old lady sleep none, either. Boy, she got pretty cranky." He laughed.

"Before she went to work this morning, she had a word for me. She told me, 'Now, you've kept me awake for three nights and I've been having to go to work every day. I'm not sick, and nobody has been doing my work for me. I've been having to do it for myself. I can't go on like we've been doing these three nights. When I come home tonight, if you haven't been to a doctor, Lebanon ain't the only place there's going to be a war going on!"

Brady's quickness to obey came as a great surprise. Whether the pain from the shoulder or fear of pain from Pauline caused his quick trip to the office may remain a mystery to me. Evidently, that war at home is something to be feared even more than the one in Lebanon.

Incidentally, after Brady's treatment, both of them slept that night.

As High As You're going

Jo Lynne always spoke her mind exactly, and she often said it bluntly. She had been a neighbor and an occasional patient of mine for several years before she accepted a position as ward clerk at the Winder-Barrow hospital. She had been married for a number of years, and yet remained childless.

When Dr. Roberts began his medical practice in Winder, Jo Lynn made several visits to his office because of some type of infection of her foot. The problem cleared fairly rapidly as she followed his advice and they began a conversational relationship whenever Dr. Roberts would make his hospital rounds.

Jo Lynn missed a couple of menstrual periods and came to my office to find out why. She appeared to be about two months pregnant, and her excitement about the news was contagious.

From my office, she drove directly to the hospital to share her news with fellow employees. My informants tell me she took the stairs two at a time in her excitement. Bursting into the nurses cubicle where she normally worked, she exuded, "I'm pregnant! I'm pregnant!"

Dr. Roberts was seated there and fumed, "It's high time your doctor knew about it."

Jo Lynn replied as only she could, "Man, you're just my foot doctor, and that's as high as you're going."

The Wrong Man?

Roman James ranked among my favorite characters. I do not remember any other black male patient who diligently cared for his father and paid immediately from his own pocket for his father's care. Roman remained consistent with this until his father's death in ripe old age. Always a courteous, clean, well dressed, family man, he consistently showed all aspects of being a model citizen,

According to evidence later presented in court, when Roman went across town, a distance of not more than two miles, he became an entirely different character. His alter-ego was a raucous, sharp-dressing, self-centered braggart who called himself, "Will King" and fathered at least one child by his lover. Will King represented everything Roman James did not—his complete antithesis.

One day, Will King entered his lover's home and found another man in bed with her. Completely enraged, he shot and killed his adversary on the spot.

To my utter amazement, the police arrested poor Roman James and charged him with the crime. The evidence against him being sufficient, he was convicted and sentenced to prison for Will King's crime.

On Roman's return from prison, apparently Will King had died. The tragedy is, Roman James essentially had died, too. He lived the remainder of his life in semi-seclusion, rarely seen except by his family.

Get Used it it, Pal

Marguerite delivered flowers for her daughter, who owned and operated a professional florist shop known as Flowers by Reba. One of the deliveries on this particular day went to a funeral home. On entering the funeral establishment, her thorough search showed no attendant in the building, although the deceased person for whom the floral offering was intended lay there on prominent display.

Marguerite's instructions were not to leave the flowers without someone signing a receipt for them, so she began to search outside the building. Finding a small boy playing just outside, she asked him, "Where are all the people who work at the funeral home?"

"Oh, dey done went to dey udder jobs," he replied.

"Well," she continued, "there's a body in there. Doesn't someone usually stay here with the body?"

"Oh, no Ma'am," came his answer. "He done dead an' he got to get used to stayin' by heself!"

Marguerite's laughter continued as she returned to the shop and gave instructions for those flowers to be delivered the following day.

Seen On TV

For a period of more than 12 years, my family operated a Christian supper club known as "The Master's Table," housed in the old First Methodist Church building, a turn-of-the-century building nearly 100 years old and of neo-Gothic architecture.

For the last three-and-one-half years of that period, we sponsored a weekly half-hour TV show called "The Paul and Bill Show." My assignment on the show each week was to tell a story, and sing a song while accompanying myself on the autoharp. The TV station claimed we had an actual audience of more than 50,000 each week as it beamed via cable throughout most of North Georgia. In all honesty, everywhere I traveled in the northern part of our state, people would recognize me and want to talk about the show.

At the height of the show's popularity, Mandy, a little girl about seven, came to my office attended by her mother. She had a sore throat. As I entered the examining room where Mandy and her mother waited, she grinned broadly as she reported, "I seen you on TV!"

Amused, I asked, "You did, Mandy? What was I doing?"

"You was a'trying to sang," came her childlike, honest reply.

What could I say? She probably had it right.

Hawaii?

The little girl, one of twins, smiled despite her earache as she came down the hallway to the examining room. "You'd better hurry," she urged. "Me and Mama are going somewhere."

"Oh, you're going somewhere?" came my questioning reply, "Alaska, maybe?"

"No, no," she smiled in reply.

"Hawaii?" continued my question.

"I'm fine," was her unexpected reply.

Waltzing back to the beginning subject after her examination and treatment, I asked, "Now where did you say you were going? Alaska?"

"No," she said.

"Hawaii?"

Again, she replied, "I'm fine."

When she returned for a recheck on her ear, I asked her Mother, "Have you told anyone what your baby said here last week?"

"Not more than a blue-million people," she responded.

This time, my Alaska-Hawaii query brought only a shy smile.

An Unusual Bat

His grandfather brought the 10 year old boy to my office with an injury involving the point of his right elbow. Swelling and bleeding into the tissue were obvious, and the slightest motion produced great pain. This kid was no wimp. X-rays confirmed he had a fracture of the olecranon process of the right ulna, the point of the elbow, just where his swelling and blueness were located.

"What position should we place his arm in when we put it in a cast? I pondered as I viewed his x-rays. If we allowed the elbow to be held at 90 degrees, the normal position for casting, it would likely distract those fragments one from the other. Yet, if the arm were extended fully, it would be awkward for the child, though the fracture fragments would tend to stay in place more easily. I chose the awkward, but better, position because it would be only for a short time. The child left my office with a plaster cast encasing his arm, and the elbow held completely straight.

Follow up visits in the office showed the cast to be causing no problem except for a tendency to slip down on the arm. The child seemed comfortable and adjusting well. Adjusting a little too well I thought when I passed the baseball field one evening fairly late. To my great dismay, there stood my patient, not as a spectator, but in the batter's box with his casted arm drawn back, waiting for a pitch.

He might not have gotten any hits with his makeshift bat before he was rudely taken out of the game, but his arm did heal perfectly.

Slow Poke

Patients had overrun my office all that day and it seemed it would never end. We had family plans for the evening, but I held to my unwritten promise to my patients: I would take whatever amount of time their problems required.

With the day nearly spent, I finally entered the room where Lorene impatiently waited. Lorene, the wife of my fishing buddy, Clyde, ranked among our best friends. We were the type of friends who could say anything to one another without worrying about silly consequence like anger.

"You are the slowest thing," Lorene complained as I entered the examination room where she waited.

Undaunted by her remark, my off-the-cuff reply even surprised me. "I'll hurry on you!" I said.

"Oh no you won't!" she objected immediately "Here I've waited while you took all that time with all those other patients and probably told every joke you have ever heard! You absolutely will not hurry with me, either."

Isn't it funny how we react when the shoe is on the other foot?

CHAPTER 13

CHURCH-RELATED AND/OR SPIRITUAL STORIES

In the practice of medicine, one deals almost exclusively with the physical and emotional sides of patients. But I believe one can be a better physician when he/she is prepared to deal with the third side of the triad—the spiritual side.

I credit two organizations for preparing me for dealing with the spiritual matters of my patients. They are the local Southern Baptist Church and the Gideons International. The training and/or experience I received in these organizations has been quite helpful and has directly or indirectly had been involved in the following stories

Southern Baptists are a high-profile organization, the largest Protestant-Evangelical unit in the world. The Gideons are well known around the world, but keep a low profile. Still, the Gideons place more than a million copies of Scripture each week, an accomplishment that brings publicity to their ministry. It comes most often in the form of humor, based on Gideons' diligence and tenacity.

Allow me to share here a small selection of stories, either funny or uplifting, from the church/spiritual side of my life:

C.B. Skelton, M.D.

A Nation Of Look-Alikes

Our Church sponsored a group of ten Cambodian refugees. It fell my lot to chair the committee helping them adjust to their new lives in America. The children were already enrolled in school and menial jobs had been secured for each of the adults. One of the men, only 19 years old, had received his first paycheck on Friday. He and I went to the local bank late that day to establish a checking account and teach him the rudiments of how to manage that account.

We were assisted at the bank by a beautiful young girl with flowing, curly, brown hair and a winsome smile. Her name was Nita. As she asked the proper questions and filled out the forms, I failed to note the impression Nita made on this young man. Apparently, his red-blooded nature had reared its head. He was awestruck.

The next morning, all ten of our immigrants loaded into a church van. I was their driver. We planned a trip to Atlanta to locate an oriental food store where they might buy the type of food more in keeping with their previous diets. I had never personally been to this store and wasn't sure where it was located. Calls to Atlanta were still long-distance at the time, so, trying to avoid the exorbitant phone charges, I planned to ask for directions at the first pay-phone where Atlanta calls were local.

We were only about six miles from Winder when we stopped at a service station to make the phone call. As I exited the van, I was followed immediately by each male Cambodian, who stayed in line directly on my heels.

About the same time, a convertible, driven by a pretty Caucasian girl with long, curly, flowing brown hair, pulled up to the service station's gas pumps. The nineteen-year-old tapped me on the shoulder and excitedly announced, "Nita! Nita!"

"No, that is not Nita. That is some other young girl whom I don't even know," I replied.

The leader of the group, then observed, "You Americans all look alike to us."

His statement taught me a needed lesson. Most of us Americans have made the same comment about other people-groups, but never think it about ourselves. What we are really saying with that comment is, "I don't care enough about this person to even distinguish their distinctive facial and body features.'

I have made an effort to change.

Calling Assured

"Oh, God, it's so far away. If we flew any farther, we would be coming back!" my silent lament rose in prayer as we flew across the Pacific Ocean on the arduous trip to Thailand. "I do hope somebody meets this plane. I won't be able to read a street sign in Bangkok nor a telephone book to find my way, if they fail to come. It has been 20 days since Mr. Goucher dictated his last letter to me. So much can happen in three weeks."

This worried musing continued throughout the arduous flight to Thailand. The trip, with layovers, spanned almost 48 hours, and I was traveling alone.

My reason for the long flight was to become a physician-volunteer in the hospital of a refugee camp for Cambodians who had sought freedom in Thailand. My church had sponsored a family of ten Cambodians and, when the call came for a volunteer 30-day replacement for a doctor on furlough, I felt certain that God led me to do it.

But, at the moment, I felt alone as never before and so uncertain about my course of action. The only things on my mind remained the distance from home to Thailand, how uncertain I felt, and how I hoped Mr. Goucher would have someone meet that plane.

As usual, my worries were without foundation. As we disembarked in Bangkok, I spotted a small hand-lettered sign saying "SKELTON" held aloft by a smiling Earl Gaucher. In my entire lifetime, only the "I love you" look on my bride's face at our wedding and, later, the tiny, wrinkled, red, squalling, faces of our newborn children and grandchildren had looked better to me and given me more comfort than that sign.

Earl and I were soon loaded in his Land Rover, headed for the missionary quarters nearly 80 miles away. Despite our animated conversation, my doubt and uncertainty still caused the question to ring in my mind, *"What am I doing here?"*

The sun had set as Earl introduced me to his wife, Dr. Joan Gaucher, who would be my boss for the next month. We entered the missionaries' quarters in pitch-black darkness because of a power failure.

As I shook a hand that grasped mine in the total darkness, I heard a voice say, "I'm Danny Hill." I mused, *Could this be the "Donnie Heel" our refugees at home have so often mentioned? They did not come through this camp. Our refugees came from the Kaoidang Camp (cow-we-dahng). But, still…I wonder.*

Further conversation with Danny revealed he had, indeed, worked at the Kaoidang Camp and that most refugees called him "Donnie Heel." He even remembered one of our refugees in Winder, Sam San, who had served as his interpreter for a short time at Kaoidang.

"Perhaps it's not such a big world as we think, is it?" questioned my newfound friend.

When Danny Hill learned of my membership in the Gideons International, he told me the following story:

"Nearly two years ago," Danny began, "the government of Thailand made a decision not to accept any more refugees. This troubled me greatly because the Gideons had provided us with 10,000 bibles in the Khmer language. Now that there would be no more refugees from Cambodia, we had no place to distribute them. I had been praying for a way to get those Bibles into Cambodia, since the Khmer Rouge had been removed from power and it was no longer a killing offense to be caught there with Christian literature.

"A few weeks later, I returned to my camp office after a weekend in Bangkok, when a young Cambodian met me at the door. 'Come quickly,' he urged. 'there is a man here I want you to meet. He is about to leave the camp and return to Cambodia,'

"He took me to meet a Cambodian pastor named Sonaan, who had walked about a hundred miles over those mine fields and come into the camp to get Bibles. He was packed for his return trip carrying six or seven of them," said Danny with obvious admiration.

"I got so excited," Danny continued, "I asked Pastor Sonaan, 'Can you meet me at the border with several of your Church members? I could bring a thousand scriptures at a time, and your people could carry them into Cambodia."

Danny smiled as he continued, "We agreed to meet in a border town called Machmun (mock-moon) at a certain date and hour. I had a thousand Gideon Bibles loaded in my Land Rover ready to go on the appointed day, when it suddenly dawned on me! I had no clearance to be in the border area. In fact, I was supposed *not* to be there. Only the Thai military and the Red Cross had that clearance.

"I prayed, 'God, if You really want me to do this, You will blind their eyes as to what I'm doing.'

'At every checkpoint, they motioned me through without question." Tears welled in Danny's eyes.

"When I arrived in Machmun, it appeared we had made a grievous error by not arranging exactly where to meet. That so called 'little town' was a city of nearly 150,000 people. Thinking my trip was a failure, I began to hand out some of the Bibles on the street. Only six or eight Bibles had been given out when this man ran up and pressed a piece of paper into my hand. When I looked at it, I saw my own handwriting. God had located me in that city of 150,000 people in just a matter of ten minutes."

By that time, I was the one with tears in my eyes.

Danny continued, "I made eight more trips and delivered a total of 9,000 Bibles to Pastor Sonaan for the people of Cambodia. Not once was I questioned. On the morning the last load was to be delivered, the Bibles were in my vehicle but I felt so low in my spirit, I could not make myself start the journey. I had never experienced anything like it before and could not begin to explain it.

"For three days, I moped and whined, thinking, 'I have let down my Lord and I have let down Pastor Sonaan and his church,' On the third day, the news came saying the Vietnamese had overrun Machmun at the exact hour I was supposed to be there. Had I, an unauthorized American missionary, been there, it could easily have been blown into an international incident, and possibly have closed our mission work in Thailand. God knows what He is doing. Sometimes, He even uses our depression to further His work."

As amazing as Danny's story sounded to me, it did not approach my even greater amazement on learning that the young Cambodian who introduced these two principal characters actually lived in a house that I owned in Winder, Georgia. Sam San Ouch was one of the ten Cambodian refugees who had been sponsored by my church.

It was as if God had allowed me to see one thread in the tapestry He is weaving. That particular thread began in Cambodia, continued through Thailand and into Winder, and I was privileged to be the shuttle loom that brought it back to Thailand.

"*It really is a small world to Him,*" I mused.

No longer feeling alone or even lonely or uncertain of my calling to Thailand, I went to work.

Aunt Mable Keeps Her Appointment

Aunt Mable's heart problems were resolving, but she remained in the hospital in Atlanta, scheduled to return home the following day. Snow covered Winder and Atlanta, and many roads in North Georgia were closed. Before we went to bed that night, Nora and I talked about how we might bring her home, since snow causes so many problems for drivers not familiar with it.

Shortly after midnight, the telephone rang, Aunt Mable's nurse bore the sad news. Our beloved aunt had suffered a cardiac arrest, but they had been able to revive her. Aunt Mable wished desperately for one of us to come.

I argued hard and finally convinced Nora that, since the roads were so bad, I should go alone. The 40 mile journey was eventually completed after quite a bit of slipping and sliding.

The nurse met me on my arrival at Aunt Mable's floor, with the message, "I'm sorry! She is already gone…but let me tell you what happened."

With tears welling in her eyes she continued, "As I told you on the phone, your Aunt Mable had a cardiac arrest. We called a Code Blue and used the defibrillator which restored her to normal heart rhythm. She immediately became able to talk to us, but your Aunt Mable was not a happy camper."

"Why did you do that?" she demanded angrily. 'I had already seen Heaven, the most beautiful place I have ever seen. I had even seen Jesus sitting at the right hand of God. Don't you ever do that again! I want to go!"

Tears were streaming down the nurse's cheeks as she continued, "When Mrs. Shurling's heart stopped again, our written orders forced us to call another Code Blue. We had no choice, so we shocked her again several more times. This time, she showed no response and I could just picture your aunt thumbing her little nose at us and saying, 'Ha ha, I got you that time. I told you before, I wanted to go."

With a story like that, we could not greatly mourn for Aunt Mable.

My Personal Parable

As a 10-year-old boy, I first heard *Flee as a Bird* sung by Molton Galloway in our little country church, accompanied on the piano by my sister, Rosa. The words of that song, but more especially the tune, rang in my boyish mind for years after that night. However, the full-impact meaning of those words seemed to elude me.

Both the words and the haunting minor-key music of *Flee as a Bird* were written by Mrs. M. S. B. Dana and published in *The Broadman Hymnal*, (© 1940, The Broadman Press, Nashville, TN).

The tune caught my imagination in a way no song had previously done. I hummed it or whistled it almost every day as I went about my work of plowing a mule on our rented farm…but without full understanding.

I later learned the title words were direct quotations from Verse One of the Eleventh Psalm but, even after reading the Scripture on which it was based, I came short of the full picture.

As I grew older, I had opportunities to sing solos in my own church and in some surrounding churches. *Flee as a Bird* naturally became one of my frequently selected songs, and people would sometimes react favorably. There were comments like, "That song is really meant for you. You do it so well."

But, even then, its simplistic meaning continued to slip my grasp. Over the years, I sang the song dozens, if not hundreds, of times and always felt there was something deeper to its message than I had ever really plumbed.

"Lord," I prayed, *"You know how I love the song and how many times I have sung it in public and private; but I still have the feeling its true, deepest meaning escapes me. I don't want to sing it anymore without a better comprehension. Please open my understanding so I can share with others the full meaning of those words. I am certain the word-picture is as beautiful as the tune."*

Shortly after that prayer, it happened.

On an absolutely fantastic and invigorating spring day, my fishing partner, Morgan Mooney, and I were in our boat on Lake Lanier near Gainesville, Ga. That day, the fish refused every offering: lures, jigs and even live minnows. We, likewise, refused to take "No" for an answer. We doggedly continued our search for fish in places where we had caught them before.

The cool west breeze felt far too refreshing, the wild azaleas and other flowers were too beautiful and sweet-smelling, and the birds' songs too melodious for us to go home now. If we stayed, we reasoned, the fish just might bite later. In the meantime, we could just enjoy the glories of nature as we continued our search for those elusive creatures.

As we positioned our boat for another drift over one of our fishing holes and bemoaned our poor fishing luck on this gorgeous day, we heard a loud, piercing scream that seemed to come from the sky. It sounded almost human—like a baby's scream.

Our gaze immediately turned skyward, and all that could be seen silhouetted against the fleecy clouds in an azure blue sky was a large hawk, swiftly moving across the lake. Suddenly, rising unexpectedly from the hawk's back, we saw a very small bird, a martin. Just as quickly as he had ascended from the hawk's back, the martin descended again in attack. The hawk screamed once more. This action was repeated several times as the Mutt-and-Jeff combatants flew South to North across the lake. The hawk screamed loudly each time the tiny martin attacked.

As the pair neared the woods on the north shore, we could hear an answering cry. We turned to see the hawk's mate coming to his rescue. Now that there were two large birds and just one miniscule martin, we wondered how the small fellow could possibly get out of this mess.

Near the north shoreline lay an abandoned, partially submerged, winding road that had been made through these mountain foothills many years before the lake was impounded. At a point near this aerial battle, a deep cut had been made for the old road, leaving a 40 foot high bank that resembled a cliff, and now formed part of the lake's north bank. The martin apparently knew this territory well and knew of a small opening in the abandoned road-bank—deep enough for him to hide—but too small for the hawks to enter. He rapidly darted into this opening leaving the two pursuing, angry hawks fluttering and chattering, begging for his blood.

I heard no audible voice as I sat there in awe, but had the distinct feeling of an inner voice saying, *"There is your answer*

"The little martin is you. One hawk represents your rebellion, your journey into the far-country, when it is fun and you are certain you can handle it. Two hawks represent the far-country journey when it has become more than you can handle and threatens to carry you away. The road-bank with its hiding place represents the mountain of God's love,

grace, forgiveness and protection where you may run and hide when you finally decide you can no longer hold your own.

"*You know the song begins 'Flee as a bird to your mountain, thou who art weary.' I am that protective mountain. You can come to Me in complete confidence of finding protection, just as that martin did!*"

We did not catch any fish that day. What I did catch—an insight into this mountain of God's love, grace, forgiveness and protection that is not off-limits to any seeker—was more thrilling, more valuable, more delectable and more life-changing than any fish I have ever caught.

From that day forward, I have felt greater understanding and no reservations with my singing of the song.

Miss Rosa And The Deacons

Miss Rosa, my mother, felt her special calling in life was to support the foreign missionaries with her prayers and finances. She had really wanted to go to the mission field, but marrying a widower with five children, then having seven of her own, precluded that inclination. She attempted to satisfy this desire of her heart by becoming president of the Woman's Missionary Union in every church where our family's depression-caused wanderings took us.

Heartbreaking results of the great depression were everywhere and Miss Rosa filled many of her days doing assorted local benevolence. The family cow might die and deprive children of life-giving milk. A cow soon appeared—given or loaned to the family. A California cousin might come to live and there was no bed for him. A bed would be found and delivered. A home might burn leaving endless needs. Basic furnishings would be found… somewhere.

Such calls were cause for Miss Rosa to spring into action, which she did with speed and wonderful success. She loved the work, but it left no time, energy or money for her "special calling" of helping to support those in foreign missions.

In frustration, Miss Rosa was heard to complain, "If the Deacons in this church carried out their duties as they should, there wouldn't be so much local charity work for the WMU. Then, we could do more toward our main job of helping support missionaries on the foreign fields."

Word travels fast in a rural community, and this word soon reached the Board of Deacons. It was not well received. They accused Miss Rosa of being disruptive to the fellowship of the church, and called a special conference to discipline her—to possibly even throw her out of the church.

My mother was never one to back down from a challenge. She felt certain her stand was correct, and showed up at the meeting with her seven-pound Scofield Reference Study Bible under her arm, already turned to the Sixth Chapter of Acts. She listened intently to the charges against her and patiently awaited her time to speak.

As she stood to defend herself, she read the Scripture in Acts Six, explaining how the early church appointed the first Deacons. "They were charged with taking care of the needs within the Church, especially the needs of widows" she preached. "You can see that clearly in the text I just read. I challenge any Deacon to show me in the Scripture where your task has changed."

Apparently her words hit their mark and had the desired results. Deacon Chairman Fred Seaforth, a kindly, robust man who filled the bib of his freshly laundered overalls as well as he filled the lower parts, stood before the gathered church body, and nervously rocked from the heels to the toes of his new brogan shoes. He admitted the Deacon Board's total lack of understanding of their responsibilities and committed them to do better in the future. He stammered, "Well, Miss Rosa's done taught me something I ain't never knowed before."

His sincere and humble response and apology continued, "I never knowed us Deacons was s'posed to do no kind of charity work! I just thought we was s'posed to take care of the business of the church, an' I have always tried to do that all the way from the firebox right on up to the steeple.

"But I can tell you one thing right now that you can count on from old Fred Seaforth as long as you keep me on this board. From here on in, I'm either gonna Deac or duck!"

Deacon Seaforth's apology appeared to be life-changing. As long as he lived, I never saw cause for him to "duck."

A Missionary At Heart

Having prevailed in her battle with the church Deacon Board, Miss Rosa continued her work with the WMU, possibly having a little more freedom to support her foreign mission causes. She absolutely thrilled upon learning of The Lottie Moon Christmas Offering for Foreign Missions. This annual offering, named after the missionary who suggested it and who literally gave her life for the people in China, became something to which my mother could really relate.

"I know I can never go and be a missionary myself,' she exulted, "but I finally have something that will help me follow my special calling. I can stay home and take care of my children, and send money to support our missionaries."

She embraced this offering and sold out to it as a yearlong project, beginning January first to gather for the December goal. Somehow, her offering had to be large, regardless of her meager circumstance.

Fried pies, cakes, cookies and donuts were made and sold by the dozens. Milk, butter and eggs were among her commodities. Handmade aprons, pincushions and many other items were fashioned and sold, all in the name of the Lottie Moon offering. As Miss Rosa lovingly laid her offering of mostly small bills and change at the altar each year, both the church and her family were amazed at its total.

Several years after the death of her beloved husband, Newton. Miss Rosa's brilliant mind became ravaged and confused by Alzheimer's

Dirty Laundry Don't Take No Doctor's Orders

Disease. Nevertheless, she continued to pursue her passion for the Lottie moon Christmas Offering for Foreign Missionaries.

She was much too proud to even consider living with one of her children. Instead, she elected to enter a nursing home, insisting she would not become a burden to anyone. Adjustment to nursing home routine was not easy because she, who had so firmly given orders for so many years, now had to take orders.

None of the family apparently gave any consideration to her passion for the Lottie Moon Christmas Offering at the time of her admission to the nursing home. Had we given it thought, chances are we would have considered it ended.

How little we knew.

My rude awakening came in the form of a telephone call from the nursing home administrator. "You need to come right away! There is a problem with Miss Rosa."

"Is she sick?" I answered, somewhat frightened.

"No, she is not sick, but there is a problem you need to help us solve. Please come quickly."

With considerable fear, I left my office for the nursing home to face…I knew not what. On my arrival, I found my mother still in full confrontation with the nursing home administrator. I had never seen her so angry.

"Your mother is breaking the nursing home rules and refuses to stop," complained the administrator. ""She has two businesses she runs to support The Lottie Moss Christmas Offering. Both of them are forbidden by our rules and must be stopped immediately. One of them has already brought harm to another one of our patients.

Slowly, the problem resurfaced. We learned that her first business was based on her in-room telephone provided by the family. Just outside Miss Rosa's room hung a pay telephone. Anyone who appeared ready to talk on the pay phone would receive a tap on the shoulder from my mother, "It will cost you a quarter to use that phone," she would say. You can use mine for only a dime."

Most of the time, The Lottie Moon Christmas Offering was increased by ten cents. This business did not bother the nursing home too badly. It was the second one that presented a special bone of contention.

Miss Rosa discerned the pride still evident in most of the resident ladies and decided to put it to Lottie Moon's advantage. Calling the local pharmacy, she asked for delivery of a bottle of hair remover, and went into the depilatory business.

"I couldn't help but notice that unsightly hair on your chin," she would say when a visitor came into her room. "I know it worries you, too. I'll take it off for just a quarter."

As soon as the fee was paid, she would apply a drop of solution to the base of the hair using a cotton-tipped applicator. The area was then massaged in a circular motion. Soon the spot was clear of unsightly hair. It worked well.

There is no way to know how many quarters went into Lottie Moon's coffers because of Miss Rosa's depilatory business. But, alas, a problem reared its ugly head.

One of her clients, a diabetic, had a minor reaction to the depilatory solution and developed a rash on her now hairless upper lip. The cat was definitely out of the bag. The nursing home had no choice but to stop this depilatory business to protect its other patients.

Now, I had to persuade Miss Rosa to give up this income for The Lottie Moon Christmas Offering. It was no easy task! I knew of no alternate suggestion except the unthinkable "Let me give you the money."

She would accept no handouts from her children even if Lottie Moon went lacking. The inviolable rule remained, she must earn it. It must cost her something.

Finally, she seemed to understand the situation and accept her fate. If she found an alternate business before God called her home, I never learned of it.

More than 20 years have passed since her death. Her dedication to her calling and her perseverance in following it still serve as beacon lights to her family and many others who knew my mother, Miss Rosa.

CHAPTER 14

Mattie

She probably ranks as the most unique among all the acquaintances of my lifetime. Stories about her have always abounded locally and, in my considered opinion, most of them are true. She had a way of causing things to happen, most of the happenings being pleasant or amusing, sometimes both. But then again, she could be terribly irritating...a plain old-fashioned nuisance. Her name was simply Mattie. In my circles as well as her own, no further name was necessary.

When our paths first crossed, I was a struggling young physician who had few patients and I willingly and eagerly took on all comers. Mattie came and, very early, it was obvious we were destined to have an interesting relationship. We estimated her age above 65 when our acquaintance began.

Mattie spoke the language typical of a southern black person of an era many years earlier, yet there somehow always seemed to be a little lilt of laughter in her voice. Many times, I think, she played me for a fool. Mischief seemed to dart about in the constant roving glances of her dark brown eyes, and it always seemed to be laced with a mysterious sense of humor. Even her "arcus senilis," a whitish, age-caused circle around the cornea, in each eye could not dim the twinkle in those devilish eyes.

Mattie had white hair with an occasional black strand, and she always kept it up in pigtails all over her head, as per the custom for most black ladies of the time. A few short hairs always seemed to seek wildly for some semblance of order.

Her face appeared excessively wrinkled, but it seemed to me, those wrinkles were caused—not so much by her age—as by her being toothless. The total absence of teeth caused her chin to rise and gave her skin less face to over. Her skin had no choice except to convolute itself and produce wrinkles. Her appearance reminded me a lot of "Mom's" Mabry.

Certainly, those wrinkles did not come from worry! Mattie never seemed to be worried, except about one thing; she had a not so secret obsession that was constantly on her mind and almost as constantly on her tongue.

It did not take long for me to uncover that obsession, so easily elucidated in her unforgettable reply to my first question. The query came simply, "Mattie, what is your problem?"

Her reply came in pitifully imperfect English and caught me in a state of total unpreparedness. "Well, Doctuh," she blurted out, "if you'll jes' listen to me, I can tell you just exactly whut's wrong wid me. I can't never get none of dese udder doctuhs to lissen but if you'll jes' set dere and give me some time, I can sho' 'nuff 'splain it to you!"

She was assured, "lissening" would be no problem for me since plenty of time lay on my hands.

She seemed to catch her breath and then continued, "Well, you see, whut's wrong wid me is, I done got caught! I'm dat way! I'm 'bout 'lebben mont' gone now."

My gasp for breath just seemed to spur her on.

"An' whut's done happen't to me is, I done fell. An' when I fell, I done knocked dat baby so hard it toined it aroun' an' it's a'kickin' an' a'pushin' an' a'tuggin' an' a'tryin to come dis a'way," Mattie continued her soliloquy as she used her hands in a broad sweep to motion upward toward her chest.

"An' whut you got to do fuh me, Doctuh," she droned on as I sat totally amazed, "you got to toin dat baby back aroun' an' make it come dat a'way like it's s'posed to come." With her concluding dramatic statement, she made another sweeping motion with her hands...downward toward her pelvis.

After partially recovering my composure, I restrained my laughter by biting my lip as I took a thorough history and did a complete physical examination on Mattie. It came as no surprise that both of these entities showed absolutely no evidence of pregnancy. X-rays were taken and even a spinal tap performed to rule out some of the less common types of brain inflammation. All of these procedures showed within normal limits and gave us no help in our diagnosis.

Of one thing we remained doubly sure; she definitely had nothing to indicate a pregnancy. Nevertheless, Mattie remained steadfast in her refusal to believe my diagnosis, but continued to come frequently to the office with the same complaint, "Dis baby is still a'kickin' an' a'pushin' an' a'tuggin.'"

She had no indication of serious illness except for her mental aberrations and, certainly, neither she nor her strange obsession posed any danger to the community. The condition is known in the medical community as "pseudocyesis." In lay terms, it means "false pregnancy." Whether her illness was classified as mental or physical, absolutely no treatment lay in my bank of medical knowledge that might help alleviate her ailment.

I strongly suspected Mattie would visit my office many times before any significant progress would be made toward resolving her complaint. A Psychiatrist might be of some help, but she remained resolute in her refusal to see anyone who practiced in that field of medicine, saying, "Is you tryin' to say I'm crazy?"

There is an old saying that states, "when rape is inevitable, relax and enjoy it."

I decided early to apply that proverb to this situation. We would humor Mattie and make every effort to enjoy the situation. My office staff received instructions to continue a policy of trying to treat any bonafide ailments she experienced and to make absolutely no effort to tamper with her notion of pregnancy. Over the next several years, this decision led to some quite interesting, and sometimes very humorous, experiences.

Whenever an opportunity presented itself, Mattie was referred to other doctors, both specialists and generalists, only to see her returned without delay to my care. We even sent her to professionals other than physicians.

When I sent her to a CPA, my sideways reasoning went like this: He is an expert on periods and deals with them all the time, even if he does call them decimal points. Mattie had certainly missed a lot of periods. Besides, a CPA can come as close to providing a cure for pseudocyesis as any general physician can.

In the natural course of events and over a period of several years, we sent Mattie to every new physician who set up a medical practice within a 30 mile radius of Winder. Our reasoning seemed logical when we sent her to ophthalmologists. "I ain't seen nothin' in 'lebben months," she had said, and she did have some vision problems associated with her advancing age.

Her unusual "pregnancy" was the obvious reason for referral to obstetrician-gynecologists. Other specialists just had to understand they were sharing a medical experience they would probably never encounter again in this lifetime—and I needed some relief!

She always came back quickly from each referral, and with no miracle cure obtained, nor even any suggestion for treatment of her unusual condition.

Soon, the "kickin' an' a'pushin' an' a'shovin'" involved not only her abdomen, but her legs and back also. In an effort to be certain I did not miss any real pathology, Mattie was put on the examining table for another complete examination. As her leg was pulled in an effort to assist her in getting further down on the examining table, to my great surprise, she expressed substantial relief of her symptoms of discomfort in the back and legs.

Dirty Laundry Don't Take No Doctor's Orders

Since we had always been absolutely unable to find any cause for her symptoms of "a'kickin an' a'pushin' an' a'shovin.'" yet had found a process that gave her partial relief from some of her symptoms, we spent several office sessions in which we both literally and figuratively "pulled Mattie's leg." For me, it was a crude concession to the chiropractic profession.

Medicare and Medicaid had not been invented in those days and Mattie had no supporting family nor any other visible means of support except for a small welfare dole. Therefore, no compensation was ever received for any of her treatment. My nurses were instructed never to be in any way rude or cruel to her, but, at the same time, not to overly encourage her visits.

She came often…and sometimes with no real purpose. On one of these seemingly purposeless visits, the office nurse asked, "Mattie, do you need to see the doctor?"

She replied, "No, Ma'am, I don't need to see him. I jes' come up here to see whut was going on." But, most of the time, Mattie wanted to talk about 'dis baby.'

During one of these visits, she informed me, "Doctuh. I think I'm near 'bout ready to be *con*fined.' meaning she thought her time for delivery of "dis baby" was near.

"Since I ain't got no money to pay no hospital bill an' I ain't got no insurance to help me," she continued "when de time come fuh me to be *con*fined, will you come to my house an' deliver dis baby?"

Knowing no delivery was forthcoming, I answered immediately, "Certainly. I'll be glad to do that, Mattie."

The thought never entered my mind that I was leaving the door open for a large problem, because absolutely no reason existed for her to ever need to be "*con*fined."

Several weeks later, sometime after midnight when sleep is the soundest and the sweetest, a loud and persistent knock at the door of my home awakened me. I slowly and begrudgingly dragged myself from the bed and drowsily opened the door. There stood the owner of one of our neighborhood grocery stores, a man who also owned a few run-down tenant houses in a small alley behind his store.

"Doc, you've got to come quick," J. L. said excitedly, "there's an old black woman who lives in one of my houses and she sure is sick with some kind of stomach trouble."

J. L. pushed aside my sleepy queries about waiting until morning as he continued, "There is just no possible way she could wait for you until morning! As sick as she is I'm afraid she might be dead before that time."

I dressed as quickly as my drowsy body would allow and followed him to the shanty where I was surprised to see the patient was Mattie. As she thrashed wildly about in her bed, she exclaimed, "Doctuh, I sho' am glad to see you. I done tole you it wuz about time fuh me to be *con*fined. Well, I wuz right. Doctuh. Dis baby is a'comin'!"

There were neither electric lights nor running water in the hovel. This shack certainly did not qualify as a place where anyone would want to do his first home delivery—not even a false pregnancy.

The dimness of light from a kerosene-lamp, could not hide the dingy color of her bed-sheets not the musty odor of filth in that house. Mattie had never had the color and appearance of being particularly unclean. How she kept from giving that impression when residing in such squalor, I could not understand.

I understood one thing perfectly. I did not want to unduly prolong my visit if there was to be any more sleep fro me before facing another full day of my now busy practice.

Mattie was examined as quickly and thoroughly as possible in these surroundings. Full consideration was given to the endless number of possible serious and less serious causes for abdominal pain, from simple gas to a ruptured peptic ulcer or a kidney stone. No illness of great consequence being found, she was given a shot for pain, some sample medicines to be used that night, a prescription for a medication for upset stomach and instructions to be seen in my office the following day.

As I hurried home to salvage whatever could be recovered from what had become a wretched night with little sleep, my resolve became complete to revoke any previous promise to deliver Mattie's "baby" at home. What reasons could I possibly give to her for this dramatic change in plans?

Suddenly the light dawned.

The next day when she came to the office, my practiced speech began. "You know, Mattie, when you deliver a baby, you absolutely have to have lots of and lots of hot water and you need a great number of perfectly clean, bleached, white towels to keep things clean and dry. When you called me to your house last night, I did not see any running water or any electricity, so I cannot figure any way you could possibly supply us with these things."

She looked a little sheepish but made no objection as I continued my tirade, "You don't want either you or your baby to get an infection or for anything else to happen that would endanger your life or this baby's life, do you?"

"Naw, suh," replied Mattie as she vigorously shook her head.

"Then, to finish the speech that I had so carefully prepared, "we will simply have to require you to deliver this baby in the hospital, just as is required of all my other patients. There can no longer be an exception to that rule, even in your case."

My sigh of relief had to be suppressed as Mattie nodded her head in assent while she pouted, "Yes, suh."

When Dr. Roberts, a young physician fresh from training in Atlanta, began his family practice in Winder, it was only natural that Mattie was immediately referred to him. I spread the mustard on right heavy as I gave her a glowing report of the wonders this highly trained God-send to our community could perform. According to the spiel I gave, he could do everything but walk on water—and he was just about one step short of accomplishing that.

Surprisingly, Mattie did not return to my office as she usually did, almost immediately after her appointment. She really appeared to like Dr. Roberts. He seemed quite patient with her as he tried to assist her in working through her problem. He even seemed to encourage her to come back to his office after she completed a considerable amount of work-up he had scheduled for her in the outpatient department of the hospital.

During this work-up, Dr. Roberts had x-rays made of her abdomen. These had already been done under my watch and had shown only normal findings of her aging. But, it was Dr. Roberts' opinion these new x-rays might help him prove to her that she was not pregnant, and wipe out the illusion that caused her delusion.

Was he evermore in for a surprise!

After the x-rays were completed, Dr. Roberts took Mattie into the x-ray consultation room at the hospital, and sat down in a chair beside her. He placed the films of her abdomen on the x-ray view-box in front of the two of them, but intentionally, he did not turn on the view-box lights. Then the Doctor began his lecture, which he hoped would be curative.

"Mattie, this is going to come as a complete surprise to you," he announced in expectant tones. "We have definite proof here that you are not pregnant! These x-rays prove that point beyond any shadow of a doubt."

Then, he repeated in even more definite tones, "You are not pregnant!"

Dramatically, he turned on the lights of the view-box, which caused the films to be illuminated. He stated firmly, "You see, there is no baby in that picture!"

Mattie bent forward almost laying her head on the table as she tried to get as close as possible to the x-rays. For what seemed to be an eternity, she intensely studied the films, pointing first to one spot on the film and then another. Eventually, she spoke.

"Well-l-l-l," she opined, staring unblinkingly at the film and never turning an eye to even glance at Dr. Roberts, "maybe from the place whur you're a'settin', you can't see it, but from the place whur I'm a'settin', I sho' can see it!"

She pointed to the lower spine area on her right side of the x-ray. Specifically, she pointed to a little wing-like bony projection off the main body of the fourth lumbar vertebra, called a transverse process. Then she noted, "Dere's his nose."

Pointing at an interspace between the fourth and fifth vertebrae, she reported, "Dere's his mouf."

Now, pointing to that interspace just above the fourth vertebra, she exulted, "Dere's his eye."

Then, she pointed to the transverse process on her left side of the same vertebra. Almost in horror, she exclaimed, "Oh, my God! Dere's anudder one jes' lak it on dat side, too! I'm a-gonna hove twins! Oh God, help me!"

Pointing in turn to the transverse process, the lower and upper interspace on her left side of the vertebra, she repeated, "Dere's his nose. Dere's his mouf. Dere's his eyes. Oh, my God!"

From that day until the day of her death, Mattie never again spoke of "dis baby," but always of "dese babies."

She returned to my care fairly soon, more certain than ever of her pregnant state. Now she even had proof!

Mary Jo was radiantly aglow as some ladies are during pregnancy. Mattie was attracted to Mary Jo, and asked her, "Ain't you gonna have a baby?"

Mary Jo answered with a smile, "Yes, I am."

"I'm gonna have some babies, too." Mattie responded patting herself on the belly.

"Dat sho' is a pretty dress you got on. Did you make it?"

Mary Jo, who had been a home economics teacher in the past, did sew beautifully. Somewhat embarrassed, she replied, "Yes, I made it."

Mattie quickly responded, "I ain't got no good-lookin' dresses like dat. Could you make me some?"

I'm not aware if Mary Jo ever entered into a sewing contact with Mattie. If she did, Mattie surely did not look as good nor ever have the radiance that we saw in Mary Jo.

For 20 or more years, Mattie and "dese babies" continued to be seen in my office without any pay. When Medicaid came on the scene, a small amount of recompense for services came along with it. However, I felt strongly that Medicaid's rulings forced me to practice a "cookbook" medicine and did not allow me to think for myself. It seemed not to allow me to consider that individuality of my patients.

When I decided to withdraw from the system, my patients were told that my love for them was greater than my love for money. They would be seen regardless of their ability to pay, as had always been my practice long before Medicaid ever existed. However, due to pressure on her from the system, this led to a separation between Mattie and me.

Not long after our forced parting, Mattie suffered a stroke and her doctor placed her in a nursing home. Even though she was under the care of another physician, we talked there from time to time as I visited my own patients in the nursing home. Her spirit seemed broken and her memory fading. The twinkle no longer remained in her dark brown eyes...a sad picture to my mind. I choose not to remember her that way.

No medical practice could survive if all the patients produced no more income than Mattie. But, I never had another patient who was nearly like her. She caused me to feel well paid in friendship, in laughter and in memories. To this date, I remember no other patient who entered the nursing home above 80 years of age, while still pregnant.

And I still miss her.

www.ingramcontent.com/pod-product-compliance
Lightning Source LLC
LaVergne TN
LVHW011945070526
838202LV00054B/4798